Basel III Liquidity Regulation and Its Implications

Basel III Liquidity Regulation and Its Implications

Mark A. Petersen and
Janine Mukuddem-Petersen

businessexpert
Press

First published in 2014 by
Business Expert Press, LLC
222 East 46th Street, New York, NY 10017
www.businessexpertpress.com

ISBN-13: 978-1-60649-872-9 (paperback)
ISBN-13: 978-1-60649-873-6 (e-book)

Business Expert Press Economics Collection

Collection ISSN: 2163-761X (print)
Collection ISSN: 2163-7628 (electronic)

Cover and interior design by Exeter Premedia Services Private Ltd.,
Chennai, India

First edition: 2014

10 9 8 7 6 5 4 3 2 1

Printed in the United States of America.

Dedicated to our daughters, Daena Blythe Kendra and Jenna Erin Dae Petersen

Abstract

Liquidity involves the degree to which an asset can be bought or sold in the market without affecting its price. The 2007 to 2009 financial crisis was characterized by a decrease in liquidity and necessitated the introduction of Basel III capital and liquidity regulation in 2010. In this book, we apply such regulation on a broad cross-section of countries in order to understand and demonstrate the implications of Basel III.

This book summarizes the defining features of the Basel I, II, and III Accords and their perceived shortcomings as well as the role of the Basel Committee on Banking Supervision (BCBS) in promulgating international banking regulation. In addition, we compare the accords in terms of their ability to determine the capital adequacy of banks and assign risk-weights to assets.

Basel III quantifies liquidity risk by using the measures liquidity coverage ratio (LCR) and net stable funding ratio (NSFR). Our book considers approximation techniques that may be applied to estimate these liquidity measures. Except for those on NSFR, our results support the rationale behind the drafting of Basel III liquidity regulation. This points to the fact that LCR regulation is far more comprehensive than that for the NSFR. We also establish that liquidity risk from the market was a more reliable predictor of bank failures than intrinsic banking liquidity risk.

Liquidity creation refers to the ability of banks to extend loans, while allowing depositors to withdraw funds on demand. The book demonstrates how to analyze the connections between liquidity creation and bank capital. We also investigate which risks liquidity creation generates for banks. In this case, we consider how Basel III regulation may be employed to manage such risks via capital and liquidity requirements. In addition, we differentiate between large, medium, and small banks to demonstrate how the effect of capital and liquidity creation differs by bank size.

The book emphasizes that the implementation of Basel III bank liquidity regulation will affect the macroeconomy of countries via intermediation costs. In particular, we quantify adjustment costs for South

African macroeconomy variables such as GDP, investment, inflation, consumption, personal income, personal savings, and employment. We find that these costs depend on the implementation period, with longer periods leading to reduced output losses. Furthermore, by comparison to the Macroeconomic Assessment Group (MAG) countries, the costs incurred are of similar size but marginally higher.

Keywords

bank failure, Basel III, capital, liquidity, liquidity creation, macroeconomic variables

Contents

List of Figures

List of Tables

Preface

Liquidity describes a bank's ability to fund asset increases and meet financial obligations, without incurring damaging losses. The 2007 to 2009 financial crisis had a negative impact on liquidity in the global banking system. The causes of the crises include excess liquidity risk, which resulted in an upsurge in credit with weak quality, excess leverage, and too little capital of insufficient quality. In response to this, new Basel III liquidity regulation was introduced. In this book, we apply such regulation on a broad cross section of countries in order to develop and demonstrate methodologies related to Basel III.

In Chapter 2, we provide an overview of the Basel I, II, and III Capital Accords as well as the role of the Basel Committee on Banking Supervision (BCBS) in promulgating international banking regulation. This includes a consideration of the history of the BCBS and its role in establishing capital adequacy for banks. Furthermore, we comment on the defining features of the Basel Accords themselves as well as their perceived shortcomings. Importantly, we make a brief comparison between the accords in terms of their capability to determine the capital adequacy of banks and assign risk-weights to assets.[1]

Basel III quantifies liquidity risk by using the measures liquidity coverage ratio (LCR) and net stable funding ratio (NSFR). In Chapter 3, we estimate the LCR and NSFR by using approximation techniques. Our results show that as the LCR increases or decreases, the probability of failure decreases or increases for both Class I (internationally active banks with Tier 1 capital in excess of $4 billion) and II (the rest) banks. This is generally in line with Basel III liquidity regulation expectations. Also, we show that as the NSFR increases or decreases, the probability of failure decreases or increases for Class II banks. However, the result that is counterintuitive is that as the NSFR increases or decreases, the probability of failure increases or decreases for Class I banks. This points to the fact that NSFR regulation still has to be improved before its implementation in 2019. We also establish that liquidity risk from the market was a more reliable predictor of bank failures in 2009 and 2010 than intrinsic banking liquidity risk.[2]

Liquidity creation refers to the function of banks to extend (illiquid) loans while providing depositors with the possibility to withdraw funds upon demand at par value. In Chapter 4, we first determine how to analyze the connections between liquidity creation and bank capital. In particular, we investigate Granger causality and its directionality between capital and liquidity creation (broad and narrow measure) in large, medium, and small banks. Second, we are interested in what risks liquidity creation generates for the bank. In a Basel III context, various aspects of such risk are taken into account by incorporating earnings volatility, credit, and nonperforming loans. Additionally, size, market share, inflation, and unemployment are included as controls. In this case, we consider how Basel III regulation may be employed to manage liquidity creation risks via capital and liquidity requirements.[3]

In Chapter 5, we emphasize that Basel III liquidity regulation will affect the macroeconomy via an increase in bank intermediation costs. If the required return on equity and cost of bank debt do not adjust, then banks will increase lending spreads to compensate for the higher cost of funding. This will negatively affect credit growth in the banking industry. Moreover, Basel III implementation will affect macroeconomic variables such as GDP, investment, inflation, consumption, personal disposable income, personal savings, and employment. In this chapter, we specifically quantify the envisaged intermediation costs for the South African economy in meeting Basel III's liquidity standards via appropriate adjustments. These costs depend on the implementation period, with longer periods leading to reduced output losses in exogenous scenarios. Furthermore, by comparison to the MAG countries, the costs incurred are of similar size but marginally higher.[4]

This book is intended for use in executive banking courses as well as advanced undergraduate, postgraduate, Masters, and MBA courses in banking; banking practitioner, consultant, and consulting seminars as well as banking libraries. The book is concise, applied, and focuses on the cutting edge topic of applying Basel III liquidity regulation. The reader will learn how such regulation relates to bank failure and capital as well as sovereign economies. In summary, the reader will benefit from this book by learning various aspects of Basel III liquidity regulation prior to its implementation.

Acknowledgments

First and foremost, we would like to thank Almighty God who has kept us and seen us throughout the years. We thank Him for his endless love, grace, favor, and blessings.

Second, we would like to express our gratitude toward our daughters, Daena and Jenna, for their support, love, and prayers while completing this book. We would like to thank the Economic Modeling and Econometrics Research Group (EMERG) for contributing to the various debates about Basel III and liquidity from 2010 onward.

Introduction

In this section, we establish the format of the main chapters of this book, namely, Chapters 3 and 5. They consist of background, results, "implications" as well as "how-to" sections.

Background Section

In Chapters 3 to 5, this subsection contains a background to the subject matter discussed in the particular chapter.

Results Sections

The key results in Chapters 3 to 5 on Basel III liquidity regulation and its connection with bank failure, capital as well as the macroeconomy are included in the main sections. This section also contains discussions on the connections with Basel III liquidity regulation.

"Implications" Section

In each chapter, the Implications section contains comments and conclusions about Basel III liquidity regulation results. This section usually comprises the following five components. We comment on connections with the background, contributions to a better understanding of the research topic, contributions to the existing knowledge, connections with the literature, and future research.

"How to Obtain the Results" Section

This section contains information on methodology involving the results and Implications sections.

CHAPTER 1

An Overview of the Basel Capital Accords

In this chapter, we provide a brief overview of the defining features of the Basel Capital Accords and their perceived shortcomings. We also, look at the role that the Basel Committee on Banking Supervision (BCBS) has to play in determining international banking regulation. The importance of capital adequacy standards is also discussed.

1.1 Background to the Basel Capital Accords

Despite their susceptibility to failure, banks fund projects and allow investment that, in turn, stimulates economic growth. Such failure can trigger economic downturns that have negative implications. As a consequence, it is important that banks are safe, and are soundly managed at all times. Banking regulation is one of the measures that can be adopted to ensure that banks remain stable. However, with an increase in globalization, cross-border banking activities are now the norm rather than the exception. This situation necessitated international regulation to ensure global banking stability.

1.1.1 Chapter 1: Main Contributions

The responses to the questions posed in the following list, provide the main issues discussed in the overview of the Basel Accords presented in this chapter:

- **Question 1.1.1 (Basel Committee for Banking Supervision)** *What is the role of the BCBS in promulgating international banking regulation ? (see Section 1.1).*

- **Question 1.1.2 (Regulatory Capital and Banking Stability)** *How can we describe regulatory capital and the part it plays in ensuring global banking stability ? (see Section 1.2).*
- **Question 1.1.3 (Basel I Features and Flaws)** *What are the defining features of Basel I and its perceived flaws ? (see Section 1.3).*
- **Question 1.1.4 (Basel II Features and Criticisms)** *What are the salient features of Basel II and the criticisms levelled at it ? (see Section 1.4)*
- **Question 1.1.5 (Basel III Features and Shortcomings)** *What are the defining features of Basel III and its anticipated shortcomings ? (see Section 1.5).*

1.1.2 The Basel Committee on Banking Supervision

Until the failure of the Herstatt Bank in Germany in 1974, individual jurisdictions made autonomous decisions about banking regulation. By then, there were several incomplete transactions between Herstatt and U.S. banks. In reality, the U.S. banks had paid Herstatt Bank in deutschmarks, but they had not received dollar payments in return. Before the aforementioned transactions could be completed, Hertstatt failed and the U.S. banks suffered large losses as a result. This incident highlighted the risks inherent in international banking and the need for coherent cross-border cooperation to negate such risks. As a consequence of the Herstatt saga, the G-10 countries (i.e., France, Germany, Belgium, Italy, Japan, the Netherlands, Sweden, the United Kingdom, the United States, and Canada) formed the BCBS under the auspices of the Bank for International Settlements (BIS). At first, this committee had the chief central bankers from each of the aforementioned G-10 member countries as its constituent members. However, other countries later joined and the BCBS currently has 27 affiliated members. It is responsible for engendering international cooperation on monetary and financial policy and operates as a central bank to BCBS affiliated central banks.[1]

The BCBS is an advisory body that deals with international banking supervision and regulation. In the main, it provides guidance on issues related to banking system stability such as capital regulation. In terms of function, after discussion with member countries, the BCBS will issue supervisory guidance and capital adequacy standards that are implemented by regulators in various jurisdictions. Collectively, these standards are called the Basel Accords, where Basel is the Swiss city where the BCBS headquarters is situated. In total, the aforementioned authority has formulated three Accords, namely, Basel I (1988),[2] II (2004)[3,4] and III (2010),[5,6] Each successive Accord was meant to be an improvement on the previous one.[7] However, the BCBS has only achieved limited success in that regard.

As BCBS operations expanded subsequent to 1974, it became apparent that international capital regulation needed to be addressed as a priority. As mentioned before, the amount of regulatory capital held is important for bank stability. Notwithstanding this, bank capital regulators in BCBS member and nonmember countries held diverse views on how to enforce capital regulation.[8]

By the mid-1980s, with an increase in cross-border banking activities, the BCBS attempted to introduce capital regulation at an international level. This, they hoped, would ensure that BCBS members and nonmembers would be protected by being subject to stringent capital requirements. In fact, in the 1980s, some large internationally active banks took advantage of the lenient capital regulation by maintaining very low capital levels. One of the exceptions to this was the United States that implemented relatively strict capital requirements during this period. By doing so, U.S. banks were at a competitive disadvantage in comparison with banks in other countries that allowed more lenient capital regulation. Such a regulatory environment created a competitive advantage for non-U.S. banks because lower capital requirements allow increased credit extension that enhances profitability.[9]

Given the aforementioned, the BCBS attempted to set standards that would harmonize bank capital regulation on a global scale. By doing so, the Committee attempted to create a more stable banking system and minimize the discrepancy in competitiveness of banks in different jurisdictions. These efforts on the part of the BCBS resulted in the adoption of the Basel I Capital Accord or Basel I entitled "International Convergence of Capital Measurement and Capital Standards."[10]

1.2 Bank Capital Regulation and Its Importance

Basel Accord regulation involves rules to ensure that banks maintain sufficient levels of capital. To understand the Basel Accords, we have to explain the concept of capital. In this regard, banks have a balance sheet (BS) that is comprised of assets, liabilities, and capital. Banks fund their assets through a combination of their liabilities and capital. Bank liabilities involve bank debt and traditionally consist of deposits. Banks' assets consist mostly of loans that provide revenue from the interest charged to borrowers. More items can be included in banks' assets and liabilities, but loans and deposits, respectively, are the most common.[11]

The difference between the total value of a bank's assets and liabilities is its capital. In reality, capital is constituted by the amount of assets not funded by debt. It follows then that if banks' liabilities exceed their assets they are considered to be negatively capitalized. When this situation occurs, a bank owes more to its debtors than it can provide from its assets and may become insolvent. In the 2007 through 2009 financial crisis, the risk of insolvency was an important issue confronting several globally systemically important banks (G-SIBs) that were considered to be too-big-to-fail. Their failure posed a systemic risk to financial sectors throughout the world. To prevent the collapse of financial systems, governments had to bail out these banks by injecting capital into them.[12]

Besides insolvency prevention, capital is important for various other reasons. First, it mitigates against credit risk that is a feature of banks' assets and involves the risk that bank loans may not be repaid. In the event of borrower default, the bank loses funds that may be owed to creditors such as depositors. In this case, it must rely on its capital to honor its obligations. Second, bank capital is important for protecting against the volatility from liabilities. Banks fund their assets through deposits that are a risk because they generally have to be made available on demand. If there is a bank run, the bank may pay such withdrawals with its capital since a bank's assets, such as loans, are illiquid. If the withdrawals are large enough, the capital may not be sufficient and the bank may become insolvent.[13]

1.3 Basel I Capital Accord or Basel I

The BCBS finalized and approved Basel I in 1988 with countries having the option to adopt its standards or not.[14] Many BCBS member and nonmember countries complied with Basel I and incorporated its features into their banking regulation. Although Basel I was intended to be applied only to internationally active banks, many countries adopted its prescripts for all banks.[15]

1.3.1 Defining Features of Basel I

Basel I utilised a capital adequacy ratio (CAR) to determine the sufficiency of capital. This ratio is the quotient of bank capital and risk-weighted assets (RWA). To be considered adequately capitalized under Basel I, a bank had to have a CAR of 8%. In formulating the CAR, the BCBS had to first define capital for regulatory purposes. Because of the differing definitions of capital, the issue caused some consternation among BCBS members. Earlier, we defined capital as the amount by which a bank's assets exceeds its liabilities. Capital can be constituted by many items, with some being more reliable than others for mitigating losses in bank assets. Under Basel I, bank capital consists of Tier 1 capital (BIT1K) and Tier 2 capital (BIIT1K).[16]

BIT1K consists mainly of high-quality core capital that has lower repayment priority in case of insolvency. As a consequence, BIT1K has a strong capacity to absorb asset losses. In turn, core capital consists mainly of common equity arising from bank ownership and includes the unencumbered common stock paid-in value as well as accumulated and disclosed retained earnings. Basel I also required that the minimum quantity of BIT1K held is 4% of RWAs.[17]

On the other hand, BIT2K is of lower quality and is mainly comprised of subordinated debt and asset loss reserves. Subordinated debt is bank-issued debts, such as bonds, that do not have to be repaid until all other creditor obligations have been met. In essence, this type of debt is subordinate to such obligations. A bank can use its proceeds from such debt issuance to honor other liabilities like demand deposits. The fact that lower quality capital like BIT2K was included in the definition of capital alludes to the fact that some BCBS member banks were not sufficiently capitalized with equity. Instead they had to rely partly on debt. In lieu of the lower quality of BIT2K, Basel I restricted the amount of BIT2K that could be included in bank capital to 100% of BIT1K.[18]

Basel I capital adequacy standards are risk based, where the required capital level is intended to be appropriate for asset-types held and their risk of loss. Here, assets with a higher chance of default should be matched by higher capital. To accomplish this, Basel I established 0%, 20%, 50%, and 100% risk categories or *buckets* into which each of the bank's assets is placed in a predetermined manner. The proportion of the asset's value included in the bank's RWA is determined by the asset category. Riskier assets were placed in higher percentage buckets, with more of that asset's value being included in the RWA. Ultimately, this translated into an increase in the bank's capital requirement.[19]

The Basel I procedure to determine the CAR also takes the risk posed by off-balance sheet (OBS) items into account. OBS items are, by definition, items held by banks that do not appear on the BS. In general, an OBS asset or liability is an item that the bank's claim to has not completely actualized. For instance, when a home equity line of credit is extended, any unused portion of that line of credit is considered an OBS bank asset. In this context, although a line of credit is a type of loan, and therefore is like an asset, the bank cannot derive benefit from any unused portion of it because there is no balance from which the bank can earn interest. Thus, OBS assets are contingent BS assets that remain OBS until a trigger occurs—for instance, a borrower draws on a line of credit—that enables the bank to profit from that asset. When an OBS asset becomes a BS asset, it carries with it a default risk just like any other asset. Bearing this feature in mind, Basel I devised a method to incorporate this risk into the CAR. To do so, Basel I created a two-step process. The first step involved applying a conversion factor to the OBS asset value. The application of this factor essentially converted the OBS asset value to take into account the probability that the OBS asset would become a BS asset.

Higher conversion factors were applied to OBS items with a higher likelihood of becoming BS items. Once the conversion factor is applied to an OBS asset, the discounted value of the OBS asset is treated like any other BS asset and placed in the appropriate risk category. This step results in the risk-adjusted value of OBS items, which is then included in the total value of the RWAs. Once all of the bank's BS and OBS assets are adjusted for risk, the values are summed. The resulting sum should equal the bank's RWAs. As before, the bank must ensure that its total capital levels (BIT1K + BIT2K) are equal to at least 8% of the bank's RWAs, with BIT1K equalling at least 4% of RWAs.[20]

1.3.2 Shortcomings of Basel I

Despite the fact that Basel I represented a first attempt to promulgate prudent bank capital regulation on a global scale, it was harshly criticized from the outset. The primary concern was related to the risk-weighting process. In particular, the Basel I bucket approach to RWAs was considered to be too general and insensitive to the idiosyncratic risks associated with each asset. In particular, each bucket contains assets with different risk levels, but because they have a common counterparty they are assumed to pose the same level of risk.[21]

This perceived problem with Basel I RWAs can be seen in the following example involving commercial loans. Under Basel I, all commercial loans are 100% risk weighted, with the bank including the entire loan value in the RWA total. Notwithstanding this, all commercial borrowers do not pose the same level of risk. For instance, in general, the risk associated with commercial loan extension to a new firm exceeds that to an established one. However, this is not reflected in the risk-weighting process, where the firms share the same risk weight.[22]

The impact of this shortcoming in risk weighting is that banks have an incentive to engage in regulatory arbitrage. Such arbitrage describes a situation where, if a bank has two options, both of which have the same risk weighting associated with them, but each of which results in differing profitability, the bank will choose the more lucrative option. In the previously mentioned commercial loan example, from a regulatory perspective, it doesn't matter whether the bank extends the loan to the new or established firm. In both cases, the bank will include 100% of the loan in its RWAs. However, from a profitability viewpoint, the loan to the new firm will be riskier, and therefore will demand a higher risk premium. Consequently, the bank will have an incentive to extend the loan to the new firm.[23]

The same principle holds true for potential borrowers within other risk categories, where no two borrowers will have the same risk profile, and yet all will be treated the same from a capital adequacy perspective. Given this situation, the bank will usually pursue the opportunity with higher profitability. However, as seen from the commercial loan example, chasing greater profitability results in higher risk. This may lead to a situation where the level of bank capital required under the Basel I methodology is not adequate for the associated risk.[24]

In summary, Basel I was criticized for its determination of the capital amount that is appropriate for the risks taken. In light of the aforementioned, BCBS members amended existing Basel I capital regulation. As a result, the BCBS document "International Convergence of Capital Measurement and Capital Standards: A Revised Framework," was produced and became known as Basel II.[25,26]

1.4 Basel II Capital Accord or Basel II

The BCBS promulgated Basel II using what is known as the "Three Pillar" approach. Here, we concentrate on Pillar I that most directly involves the calculation of capital adequacy. This Pillar also clearly attempts to respond to the criticisms of Basel I. On the other hand, Pillars II and III, dealing with supervisory review standards and market discipline issues, respectively, do not intimately involve CAR calculation.[27,28]

1.4.1 Defining Features of Basel II and Differences from Basel I

Before we proceed, we note what portions of Basel I remain unchanged in Basel II. Basel II still requires that a bank's regulatory capital equal to be at least 8% of its RWAs. It also still assesses capital adequacy using the CAR. Basel II did not change the definition of capital from Basel I. However, Pillar I in Basel II amends the calculation of RWAs. Because Pillar I addresses problems with Basel I, it attempted to change the methodology associated with credit risk measurement.[29,30] The intention was to align the calculation of perceived risk in a bank's assets to the actual risk. It was hoped that this would reduce regulatory arbitrage, one of the primary deficiencies of Basel I. Pillar I measures credit risk via the Standardized (S) Approach, Foundation Internal Ratings-Based (FIRB) Approach, and the Advanced Internal Ratings-Based (AIRB) Approach.[31,32]

The S Approach from Basel II is the simplest of the aforementioned approaches and most similar to that of Basel I. It is suitable for smaller banks. In this approach, risk-adjusted asset values are also determined by using risk buckets. However, the S Approach from Basel II treats risk weighting differently from Basel I in the following ways. First, the S Approach considers six instead of four risk buckets. In addition to the Basel I 0%, 20%, 50%, and 100% risk categories, this approach adds 150% and 35% risk categories with the latter catering for residential mortgage loans. The next difference between the S Approach and Basel I involves the process of allocating assets to risk buckets. We recall that under Basel I, assets were allocated based on the counterparty's identity. Since different assets have different risk profiles, the S Approach from Basel II determined risk weightings based on idiosyncratic risk features of individual bank assets. In order to achieve this, Basel II's S Approach uses counterparty ratings from credit-rating agencies (CRAs), such as Standard & Poor's (S&P) and Moody's to assign assets to risk buckets.[33,34]

Under S Approach prescripts, there is a negative correlation between counterparty ratings and risk bucket categories. For instance, if a commercial borrower receives a high (for instance, AAA, where an obligor rated "AAA" has an extremely strong capacity to meet its financial commitments. AAA is the highest issuer credit rating assigned by S&P) rating, the associated loan would be placed in a low (for instance, 20%) risk bucket. By contrast, regardless of the creditworthiness of the borrower, Basel I placed all such commercial loans in the 100% risk bucket.[35]

For unrated borrowers, the S Approach from Basel II automatically places that loan in the 100% risk bucket. The S Approach makes an exception for the credit rating of residential mortgage loans that are assigned to the 35% risk-weighted category automatically. Under the S Approach, asset risk-weighting depends not only on credit ratings, but also on whether that asset involves a sovereign claim. Under the premise that government assets are less risky, the S Approach assigns such credit rated assets to a lower risk category than an asset that represents a private party claim, even if their credit ratings are equal.[36,37] For instance, a S&P AAA-rated government asset would be risk weighted at 0%, whereas an AAA-rated business loan would receive a risk weight of 20%.

The FIRB and AIRB Approaches are more suited for larger and more sophisticated banks. The main difference between the S Approach and the two Internal Ratings-Based (IRB) Approaches is that with the latter, banks utilize internal methods to determine asset risk levels. By contrast, with the S Approach, banks must rely on external ratings to risk-weight their assets. In order to receive regulatory approval, if banks use the sophisticated IRB Approaches, they must possess the technical ability to implement them.[38]

To understand the IRB methodology, one must develop an appreciation of the concept of unexpected losses. These losses are unforeseen and essentially approximate credit risk. Banks can anticipate and prepare for expected losses by looking at historical loss rates. Banks hold loan-loss reserves to provision for such losses. On the other hand, when banks incur unexpected losses they need capital to cushion the blow. To estimate a bank's unexpected losses, four inputs are used in the FIRB and AIRB Approaches. The first input is the probability of default (PD) that provides an estimate of the probability over a one year period that a given borrower will default. The next input is the loss given default (LGD) that involves an estimate of the losses when borrowers default. Since banks usually recover some amount from the borrower, the LGD comprises the bank's net loss. The third input is the exposure at default (EAD) that represents the additional amount that a bank could lose at the time of borrower default. An example would be the unused portion of any credit line available to a defaulting borrower, where the borrower still has the ability to draw on the line, thereby creating additional assets for the bank that can also go into default. The final input is the asset maturity (M) or duration of the loan. The higher the M value, the larger the likelihood of borrower default. Therefore, *ceteris paribus*, long maturity assets lead to a higher asset risk weighting. After the PD, LGD, EAD, and M are calculated, models are used to estimate the bank's unexpected losses or credit risk.[39,40]

Differences between the FIRB and AIRB Approaches hinge on the determination of the input values. Under the FIRB Approach, a bank calculates the PD for each asset, while the LGD and EAD are determined by the bank's regulator. With regard to M, the regulator has the discretion to assign an estimated maturity to each asset or allow the bank to make its own calculations. However, the AIRB Approach allows banks to calculate the values for PD, LGD, EAD, and M. If a bank is allowed to use either IRB Approach, its methodology and outputs must be ratified by regulators. With both Basel II IRB Approaches, banks have carte blanche to decide on the actual model to estimate their credit risk level. Regardless of how a bank accomplishes this, its calculation will be used to determine the extent to which the asset value will be included in the bank's RWAs.[41]

When compared with Basel I and the S Approach, the IRB Approaches seemingly provide an enhanced ability to determine actual risk. In this regard, instead of the broad risk-insensitive buckets from Basel I and the S Approach, the IRB models assign risk weightings in an asset-specific manner. Moreover, the IRB Approaches should result in a more accurate risk assessment because banks, with an intimate knowledge of their customers, are left to calculate risk levels themselves.[42,43]

1.4.2 Shortcomings of Basel II

In the S Approach, the first shortcoming of Basel II is related to the use of CRAs to determine an asset's risk. Because these agencies are remunerated by those they are supposed to rate, conflicts of interest arose. An example of a problem with CRAs was their inability to warn against the dangers of securitization that did so much damage before and during the 2007 to 2009 financial crisis. Under the S Approach of Basel II, all securitized product exposures by a bank would be assigned a risk weight. However, this assignment depends on an external credit rating. As a consequence, CRAs play a vital role in determining the amount of bank capital held in order to mitigate the risks from securitization.[44,45]

As the subprime mortgage crisis showed, many CRAs assigned inappropriately high ratings to securitized products. There are two reasons for this. First, many CRAs relied on inadequate rating processes to assess risks from securitization. Second, because CRAs were being paid by those they were rating, concerns arose regarding the reliability and objectivity of the ratings they provided. Thus, because the risk of securitized exposures was perceived to be low, as indicated by the high credit ratings, banks held insufficient capital in relation to the real risk associated with such products. As a result, when the underlying assets (particularly, subprime mortgage loans) of the securitized products defaulted, banks did not have enough capital of suitable quality to absorb securitization exposure losses.

Another concern about the S Approach is the lack of a uniform rating system. Basel II does not prescribe which CRA a bank must use. So banks can employ various CRAs that assign ratings in different ways. Under this regime, credit risk assessment across banks is not consistent. Critics also point out that the S Approach does an inadequate job of differentiating risk among unrated borrowers, where it simply assigns such borrowers a 100% risk rating. Thus, the S Approach shares the same criticisms with Basel I, where borrowers of varying degrees of risk are included in the same risk category.[46]

Although the IRB Approaches appear to be an improvement on previous attempts to assess risk, they also have their flaws. For instance, problems have been encountered with the fact that such approaches assess risk internally. This leads to a lack of consistency among different banks with the same asset inputs, but different risk-assessment models. Under the IRB regime, bank regulators scrutinizing these approaches have an increased responsibility to ensure that the assessments of internal risk are reflective of the actual situation. Because of the complex internal risk-assessment processes followed by banks, this may lead to an unhealthy dependence of bank regulators on risk information provided by the banks themselves. This situation is tantamount to self-regulation.[47]

Another criticism levelled at IRB Approaches is that they are inclined to encourage procyclical behavior by banks. In essence, such approaches tend to promote the holding of less capital during economic booms when borrowers are more likely to honor their debts. On the other hand, banks act in a malevolent way during busts when striving to hold sufficient capital to cover unusually high asset losses. In reality, such procyclical bank behavior could result in inappropriately lower asset risk assessments. As a consequence, IRB models would underestimate the amount of capital required to be held during booms. However, during stress scenarios when credit risk is enhanced, the IRB Approaches would reflect higher risk levels. This would result in an increase in the bank's RWAs as well as its capital requirement. As a result, banks would have to provision for the periods when they maintain low capital levels. To accomplish this, banks would have to decrease loan extension to improve their CAR. This situation may lead to a credit crunch that worsens the severity of economic crises. The reason for this is that if banks curb loan extension, the funding of economic activity is restricted and growth becomes impaired. As a consequence, economic recovery efforts are stunted. During the 2007 through 2009 financial crisis, this phenomenon had a devastating impact on the global economy. For instance, banks holding low-quality subprime mortgage loans had to reduce loan extension to prevent their CAR from decreasing too much.[48]

The flaws in Basel II were identified prior to the 2007 to 2009 financial crisis. In reality, at the outset of the said crisis, the BCBS had already begun preparations to improve Basel II. However, the widespread devastation caused by the crisis hastened the need for Basel II to be revised. In September 2010, the BCBS released the latest version of the Basel Accords in the form of the Basel III Capital and Liquidity Accord or Basel III.[49,50]

1.5 Basel III Capital and Liquidity Accord or Basel III

The BCBS augmented Basel II by launching the Basel III Capital and Liquidity Accord in the form of the document "A Global Regulatory Framework for More Resilient Banks and Banking Systems," in September 2010.[51,52] Basel III encapsulates attempts by the BCBS to take the lessons learned from the 2007 to 2009 financial crisis to inform international banking regulation. The objective of Basel III was to enhance the ability of banks to absorb asset losses without negatively affecting sovereign economies. In terms of bank capital regulation, Basel III strives to optimize the quantity and quality of capital.

1.5.1 Defining Features of Basel III and Relationship With Basel II

Basel III redefines regulatory capital to make it more restrictive and increase its quality. Like Basel I and II, Basel III also differentiates between T1K and T2K. In the sequel, we denote Basel III T1K and Basel

III T2K by BIIIT1K and BIIIT2K, respectively. However, in Basel III, such capital is constituted by higher quality components than that of the other Accords. Therefore, potentially it is able to absorb asset losses more effectively. Under Basel III, BIIIT1K consists mainly of core capital that is made up of common equity and retained earnings. Moreover, some BIIIT2K items included in capital calculations under Basel II—for instance, subordinated debt—will not be included under Basel III.[53,54]

As with Basel I and II, under Basel III, banks must maintain a minimum total CAR of at least 8% of RWAs by the time of full implementation of Basel III in January 2019. However, under the latest Accord, in addition to the 8% capital requirement, banks will have to hold a minimum capital conservation buffer of 2.5% of RWAs. The purpose of this buffer is to ensure that banks have sufficient capital levels to absorb asset losses, especially during stress scenarios. This means that the capital requirement totals 10.5% of RWAs.[55]

Besides improved capital quality, Basel III also prescribes an increase in the quantity of BIIIT1K that banks are required to hold. Under this Accord, banks should hold a minimum quantity of BIIIT1K equal to 6% of RWAs. This represents a 2% increase over the BIIT1K requirement of 4%. Furthermore, banks will have to hold a minimum amount of core capital of 4.5% of RWAs. Under Basel I and II, core capital had to represent only 2% of RWAs. By comparison to the other Basel Accords, the total core capital-to-RWAs that banks are required to hold under Basel III increases to 7%. This amount includes the capital conservation buffer that is also constituted by core capital.[56,57]

To counteract procyclicality, Basel III requires banks to maintain a countercyclical buffer of 0% to 2.5% of RWAs. The exact size of the buffer will be determined by the level of credit extension in any given economy with higher credit growth requiring a higher buffer. This buffer is designed to ensure that banks hold sufficient capital in times of excessive credit growth. This situation usually arises when assets are perceived to carry low risk. In essence, the countercyclical and capital conservation buffers are closely related in that they both counteract low capital levels in periods of low perceived risk. As a result, by holding elevated capital levels during booms, banks can avoid deleterious measures to conserve capital during busts. This will hopefully prevent credit crunches. If we suppose a countercyclical buffer of 2.5%, Basel III could potentially require banks to exceed a capital-to-total RWAs ratio of 13%.[58]

When it issued Basel III, the BCBS indicated that it would collaborate with the Financial Stability Board (FSB) to enforce especially high capital requirements for SIBs. The BCBS stated that these capital requirements for SIBs would mainly be constituted by contingent capital, capital surcharges, and bail-in debt. Unlike the BCBS, the FSB sets regulator standards not only for the banking industry but the entire financial sector. Like the BCBS, the FSB is an international body consisting of financial regulatory authorities from various countries.[59]

Basel III introduces a leverage ratio that will require banks to hold a minimum capital-to-total assets ratio of 3% regardless of the risk associated with the assets. By requiring a leverage ratio, Basel III restricts the evasion of minimum capital requirements by banks. Thus, the leverage ratio is intended to ensure that banks hold some capital to provision for unexpected losses.[60]

The Basel III implementation timeline mitigates against forecasts that elevated capital requirements will damage economies and decrease profitability. In this regard, Basel III will only be fully implemented by the beginning of 2019. This timeline provides banks with the opportunity to adapt to increased capital requirements and allow for a seamless transition from Basel II to Basel III.[61,62]

1.5.2 Overview of Basel III

In this section, we provide an overview of Basel III capital and liquidity regulation.[63] In this regard, we present the key components of the aforementioned regulation in Figure 1.1.

The key elements of Basel III capital and liquidity regulation in Figure 1.1 are explained in the sequel. In so doing, we also outline the major differences between Basel II and Basel III regulation.[64,65]

As we have noted before, Basel III augments Basel II by strengthening Pillar 1 with enhanced minimum capital and liquidity requirements (in Figure 1.1 see **(A1)** and **(A3)**, respectively). Pillar 2 (supervisory review) and Pillar 3 (market discipline) are the same as for Basel II (see **(A4)** and **(A5)** in Figure 1.1). Further information is given in the following paragraphs.

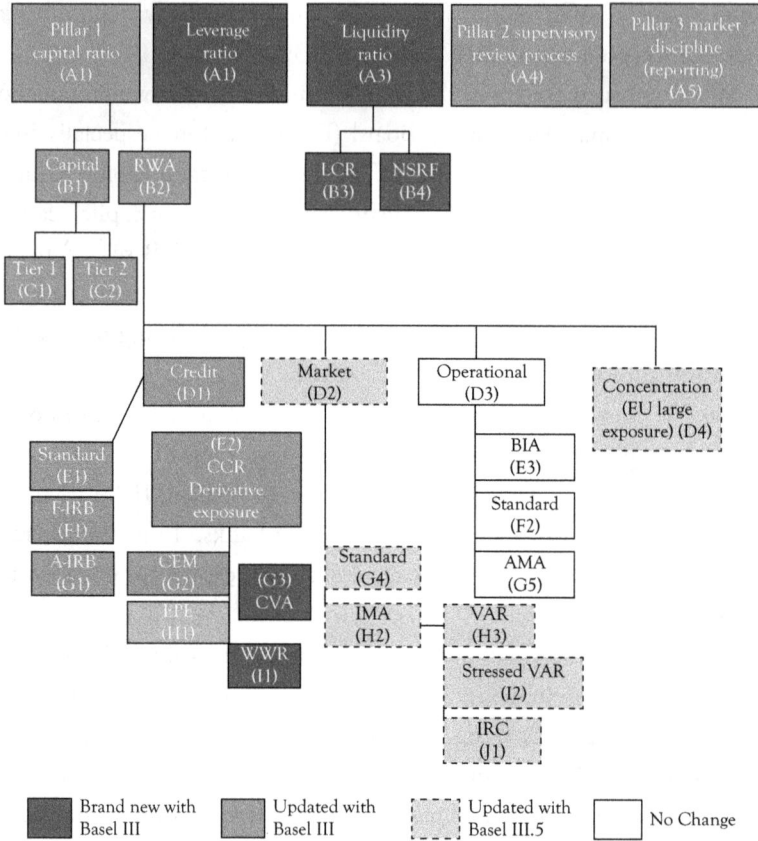

| Pillar 1 capital ratio (A1) | Leverage ratio (A1) | Liquidity ratio (A3) | Pillar 2 supervisory review process (A4) | Pillar 3 market discipline (reporting) (A5) |

Capital (B1) — RWA (B2)   LCR (B3) — NSRF (B4)

Tier 1 (C1) — Tier 2 (C2)

Credit (D1) — Market (D2) — Operational (D3) — Concentration (EU large exposure) (D4)

Standard (E1) — (E2) CCR Derivative exposure   BIA (E3)

F-IRB (F1)   Standard (F2)

A-IRB (G1) — CEM (G2) — (G3) CVA — Standard (G4) — AMA (G5)

EPE (H1)   IMA (H2) — VAR (H3)

WWR (I1)   Stressed VAR (I2)

IRC (J1)

Legend:
- Brand new with Basel III
- Updated with Basel III
- Updated with Basel III.5
- No Change

Figure 1.1 Overview of Basel III capital and liquidity regulation

First, the new capital standards and buffers will require banks to hold a higher quality and quantity of capital than under Basel II (see **(A1)** in Figure 1.1). Increasing capital ratios (BIIIT1K, BIIIT2K, TK, conservation buffer, countercyclical buffer), stricter rules on eligible capital, and higher capital requirements (RWAs increase for some asset classes) should be beneficial (see **(B1)**, **(C1)**, and **(C2)** in Figure 1.1).[66]

Second, Basel III enhances risk coverage by strengthening the capital and risk management requirements for counterparty credit risk (CCR) exposures arising from derivatives, repos, and securities financing activities (SFAs). For example, Basel III calculations depend on inputs during stress scenarios, although wrong way risk (WWR) and credit value adjustment (CVA) risk are explicitly included (see **(G3)** and **(I1)**). Also, the proposed regulation increases CCR capital for trades with financial institutions (see **(E2)** in Figure 1.1). This includes capital charges for mark-to-market (MtM) losses (CVAs and CVA risks) and WWR as well as stress expected positive exposure (EPE) (see **(G3)**, **(I1)**, and **(H1)**). The technique employed here involves the current exposure method (CEM) as presented in **(G2)** in Figure 1.1.[67]

In the third place, Basel III introduces LRs that are a nonrisk based measure to supplement the risk-based minimum capital requirements (see **(A1)**). This ratio aims to assist in containing the accumulation of excessive leverage by introducing measures to curb the manipulation of risk-based requirements and address model risk. Basel III aims at raising the quality of the capital to place banks in a position to better absorb operational losses, monitor leverage (see **(A2)**), and improve bank liquidity (see **(A3)**, **(B3)**, and **(B4)** in Figure 1.1.).[68,69]

Fourth, Basel III attempts to reduce cyclicality and promote countercyclical buffers. The countercyclical framework is intended to encourage the building of capital buffers.[70]

Finally, Basel III introduces a global minimum liquidity standard for internationally active banks that include the 30-day liquidity coverage ratio (LCR) requirement and longer term net stable funding ratio (NSFR) (see **(A3)**, **(B3)**, and **(B4)**).[71,72] In addition, Basel III outlines a set of standard liquidity monitoring metrics to improve cross-border supervisory consistency. This involves a common set of monitoring metrics to assist supervisors in identifying and analyzing liquidity risk trends at the bank and at a system-wide level to better anticipate risks from systemic disruptions (see **(A3)**, **(B3)**, and **(B4)** in Figure 1.1).[73]

1.5.3 Shortcomings of Basel III

A first shortcoming of Basel III involves the capital level that banks are required to maintain. It is anticipated that prescribed Basel III capital levels will have a negative impact on credit extension and thus economic growth. In this regard, an Institute of International Finance (IIF) report claims that Basel III requirements would result in a 3.1% decrease in gross domestic product (GDP) for every 1% increase in CAR. On the other hand, a report produced by the BIS concluded that GDP would decrease moderately by 0.09% for every 1% increase in CAR.[74]

It is envisaged that Basel III will negatively affect bank profitability. In essence, banks will compensate for the loss of income from reduced credit extension by increasing the interest rates charged on loans. This will make credit more expensive and incentivize banks to hold riskier assets despite elevated capital requirements.[75]

An opposite standpoint to this one about Basel III capital requirements is that capital requirements are still too low to ensure effective loss absorption during stress scenarios such as those experienced in the 2007 through 2009 financial crisis. The claim is that many banks that became distressed during the aforementioned crisis maintained capital levels that exceeded Basel III requirements. Some studies even suggest that Basel III capital requirements should be twice as big as what they are at present.

Another point of view is that Basel III does not properly address the shortcomings of Basel II. For example, Basel III does not improve on Basel II processes for allocating risk to assets. In particular, the latest Accord does not improve the Basel II RWA calculation and address the problem of using CRAs to determine bank risk. Basel III also fails to align the IRB Approaches to counteract the use of different risk-weighting methodologies in the banking industry. The consensus is that Basel III has improved the constituents of capital, but failed to address the problems related to risk weighting.[76,77]

1.6 Implications of the Basel Accords

International banking regulation has changed significantly since the forming of the BCBS in 1974. In the wake of Basel I[78] and II[79,80], as the 2007 to 2009 financial crisis has shown, capital regulation still has to improve. Basel III[81,82] has made a valiant effort to achieve this but may merely be one of many attempts to improve international banking regulation.

CHAPTER 2

Introduction to Basel III Liquidity Regulation

Liquidity involves a bank's ability to fund assets and honor liabilities without incurring major losses. Because of the maturity transformation of short-term deposits into long-term loans, banks are susceptible to liquidity risk of an idiosyncratic and market-wide nature.[1,2]

The 2007 to 2009 financial crisis re-emphasized the key role that liquidity plays in the financial and banking sectors.[3] Before the crisis, financial markets were bullish and low cost funding was easy to acquire. The reversal in market conditions thereafter led to a reduction in global liquidity for several years. Banks suffered severe pressure that resulted in central banks and regulatory bodies undergirding the operations of markets and financial institutions.[4]

In responding to the crisis, the Basel Committee on Banking Supervision (BCBS) and its subgroup, the Working Group on Liquidity (WGL), announced a strengthening of the international banking regulation via the Basel III Capital and Liquidity Accord on Sunday, September 12, 2010.[5,6] In the main, this banking accord is a regulatory standard on capital adequacy, stress testing,[7] and market liquidity risk. More specifically, the rationale was that Basel III would negate the deleterious effects of liquidity shocks on credit extension.[8]

2.1 Preliminaries on Liquidity Classification

Table 2.1[9] is adapted from Horvath et al.[10] and summarizes the Bouwman–Berger liquidity classification of balance sheet (BS) and off-balance sheet (OBS) items that will be referred to subsequently in our study of liquidity creation in Chapter 4.

Table 2.1 Liquidity classification of balance sheet (BS) and off-balance sheet (OBS) items and their weights

Assets		
Illiquid assets (weight 0.5)	**Semi-liquid assets (weight 0)**	**Liquid assets (weight −0.5)**
Financial assets held for trading with maturity > 1 year	Financial assets held for trading with maturity between 3 months and 1 year	Financial assets held for trading with maturity < 3 months
Financial assets designated at fair value through profit or loss with maturity > 1 year	Financial assets designated at fair value through profit or loss with maturity between 3 months and 1 year	Financial assets designated at fair value through profit or loss with maturity < 3 months
Available-for-sale financial assets with maturity > 1 year	Available-for-sale financial assets with maturity between 3 months and 1 year	Available-for-sale financial assets with maturity < 3 months
Loans and receivables with maturity > 1 year	Loans and receivables with maturity between 3 months and 1 year	Loans and receivables with maturity < 3 months
Held to maturity investments with maturity > 1 year	Held to maturity investments with maturity between 3 months and 1 year	Held to maturity investments with maturity < 3 months
Derivative-hedge accounting (positive fair value) with maturity > 1 year	Derivative-hedge accounting (positive fair value) with maturity between 3 months and 1 year	Derivative-hedge accounting (positive fair value) with maturity lower than 3 months
Other assets with maturity > 1 year	Other assets with maturity between 3 months and 1 year	Other assets with maturity lower than 3 months
		Cash and cash balances with Central Banks
Liabilities		
Illiquid liabilities (weight −0.5)	**Semi-liquid liabilities (weight 0)**	**Liquid liabilities (weight 0.5)**
Financial liabilities held for trading with maturity > 1 year	Financial liabilities held for trading with maturity between 3 months and 1 year	Financial liabilities held for trading with maturity < 3 months
Financial liabilities designated at fair value through profit or loss with maturity > 1 year	Financial liabilities designated at fair value through profit or loss with maturity between 3 months and 1 year	Financial liabilities designated at fair value through profit or loss with maturity < 3 months

(Continued)

Table 2.1 (Continued)

Financial liabilities measured at amortized cost with maturity > 1 year	Financial liabilities measured at amortized cost with maturity between 3 months and 1 year	Financial liabilities measured at amortized cost with maturity < 3 months
Derivative-hedge accounting (negative fair value) with maturity > 1 year	Derivative-hedge accounting (negative fair value) with maturity between 3 months and 1 year	Derivative-hedge accounting (negative fair value) with maturity < 3 months
Other liabilities with maturity > 1 year	Other liabilities with maturity between 3 months and 1 year	Other liabilities with maturity lower than 3 months
		Deposits, loans, and other financial liabilities vis-à-vis Central Banks
Off-Balance-Sheet Items		
Illiquid items (weight 0.5)	**Semi-liquid items (weight 0)**	**Liquid items (weight −0.5)**
Commitments and guarantees given with maturity > 1 year	Commitments and guarantees given with maturity between 3 months and 1 year	Commitments and guarantees given with maturity < 3 months
Commitments and guarantees received with maturity > 1 year	Commitments and guarantees received with maturity between 3 months and 1 year	Commitments and guarantees received with maturity < 3 months

2.2 Preliminaries on Basel III and Traditional Liquidity Risk Measures

The "Sound Principles"[11] BCBS document intends to promote improved liquidity risk management. To complement these principles, the BCBS has introduced the two minimum liquidity standards, namely, liquidity coverage ratio (LCR) and net stable funding ratio (NSFR). The upholding of the LCR and NSFR standards is crucial for the success of Basel III.[12]

In particular, the LCR aims to mitigate liquidity stress scenarios over a 30-calendar day period. This liquidity risk measure forces banks to hold adequate levels of unencumbered high-quality liquid assets (HQLAs) that are meant to counterbalance net cash outflows experienced during short-term liquidity implosions.[13–15] The application of the LCR involves both institution-specific and systemic shocks.[16] On the other hand, the

NSFR intends to promote longer term funding of bank assets and activities by establishing a minimum stable funding standard over a one-year horizon.

In the sequel, we also consider traditional liquidity risk measures such as the nonperforming assets ratio (NPAR), return on assets (ROA), London Interbank Offered Rate overnight indexed swap spread (LIBOR-OISS), Basel II total capital ratio (BIITKR), government securities ratio (GSR), and brokered deposits ratio (BDR). These risk measures will be defined later in this chapter in Subsection 2.2.3.

2.2.1 Liquidity Coverage Ratio

The LCR attempts to ensure an adequate stock of unencumbered HQLAs that consist of liquid assets that can be converted in markets into cash with minimal value loss and are subject to a range of haircuts.[17–19] These assets are of the highest quality and most liquid.

2.2.1.1 Description of the LCR

The LCR specifications follow directly from several Basel documents on liquidity that are quoted in the text. The LCR has two components: (a) total stock of HQLAs as a numerator and (b) total net cash outflows (NCOF) as a denominator. The LCR is expressed as

$$LCR = \frac{\text{Total Stocks of HQLAs}}{\text{NCOF Over the Next 30 Calendar Days}}. \qquad (2.1)$$

In the absence of banking stress, the LCR standard requires that an ongoing minimum value of 100% be maintained. During periods of liquidity stress, however, banks are allowed to use their stock of unencumbered HQLAs, and drop below the 100% standard.[20,21]

In order to qualify as a HQLA, an asset should be liquid in markets during short-term stress scenarios and be eligible for use in interventions by central banks. HQLAs are comprised of Level 1 assets (L1As) and Level 2 assets (L2As). More specifically, L1As include cash, central bank reserves, and certain marketable securities backed by sovereigns and central banks.

In order to meet the LCR standard, there is no limit to the extent to which a bank can hold these assets. Also, L2As consist of Level 2A assets (L2AAs) and Level 2B assets (L2BAs). L2AAs include, for instance, certain government securities, covered bonds, and corporate debt securities. On the other hand, L2BAs are constituted by lower rated corporate bonds, residential mortgage-backed securities, and equities that meet certain conditions. According to Basel III, in aggregate, L2AAs and L2BAs should account for less than 40% and 15% of HQLA stock, respectively.[22]

Total NCOF constitutes the LCR denominator and is defined as the total expected cash outflows minus total expected cash inflows during the specified 30-day stress scenario. In turn, total expected cash outflows are determined by multiplying the outstanding balances of various categories of liabilities and OBS commitments by the rates at which they are expected to run off or be drawn down. Moreover, total expected cash inflows are calculated by multiplying the outstanding balances of various categories of contractual receivables by the rates at which they are expected to flow in. Total cash inflows are subject to an aggregate cap of 75% of total expected cash outflows, thereby ensuring a minimum level of HQLA holdings at all times.[23]

2.2.1.2 Implementation of the LCR

In January 2013, the BCBS's final LCR prescripts were endorsed by its governing body, the Group of Central Bank Governors and Heads of Supervision (GHOS).[24] As illustrated in Table 2.2,[25] the LCR will be introduced on Thursday, January 1, 2015, but the minimum requirement will begin at 60%, increasing in equal yearly increments of 10% to reach 100% by Tuesday, January 1, 2019. This incremental implementation schedule allows for the introduction of the LCR standard with as little disruption as possible. Here, the BCBS would like to ensure the strengthening of banks in an orderly manner and ongoing finance for economic activity.

Table 2.2 Implementation of minimum LCR requirements (2015–2019)

Years	2015	2016	2017	2018	2019
Minimum LCR Requirement	60%	70%	80%	90%	100%

2.2.1.3 Illustrative Example of the LCR

By way of illustration, we determine the LCR for Bank A that holds six asset types, namely, cash, reserves, Treasury securities, government, and corporate bonds as well as retail loans. In particular, reserves and Treasuries are L1As, and we suppose that corporate bonds are L2As. Bank A funds itself using a combination of unsecured wholesale funding, overnight interbank borrowing, stable and less stable deposits, borrowings from the Central Bank as well as equity. Table 2.3 presents the BS item values[26,27] for our example.

The stock of HQLAs for LCR purposes is given by

$$A^{HQL} = C + R + T + B^G + \min[0.85 * B^C, \tfrac{2}{3} * (C + R + T + B^G)] = 267$$

$$(2.2)$$

For the different types of liabilities, the funds outflow associated with stress scenarios depend on the run-off rates specified by LCR prescripts.[28] If θ^j denotes the run-off rate for liabilities of type j and O^C denotes contractual outflows with $O^C = 10$, it follows that:

$$O = \theta^{D^S} D^S + \theta^{D^L} D^L + \theta^{F^U} F^U + \theta^{B^I} B^I + \theta^{B^C} B^C + O^C \qquad (2.3)$$

$$= 0.075 \times 150 + 0.15 \times 150 + 0.75 \times 210 + 1 \times 80 + 0.25 \times 50 + 10$$

$$= 306.25.$$

Here the run-off rate for stable retail deposits, less stable retail deposits, and unsecured wholesale funding are taken to be 7.5%, 15%, and 75%,

Table 2.3 Illustrative balance sheet for computing LCR

Assets		Liabilities	
Cash (C)	50	Stable Retail Deposits (D^S)	150
Reserves (R)	25	Less Stable Retail Deposits (D^L)	150
Treasuries (T)	50	Unsecured Wholesale Funding (F^U)	210
Government Bonds (B^G)	100	100 Interbank Borrowings (B^I)	80
Corporate Bonds (B^C)	50	Central Bank Borrowings (B^C)	50
Retail Loans (Λ)	425	Equity (E)	60
Total	700	Total	700

respectively. Here, the run-off rates on overnight interbank borrowing and secured transactions with the Central Bank against non-HQLA is 100% and 25%, respectively. If we suppose that contractual inflows is 6, the expected net cash outflow is given by

$$O^{NC} = 306.25 - \min(6, 0.75 * 267.5)$$

$$= 306.25 - \min(6, 200.625) \tag{2.4}$$

Hence, the LCR, C^{Lr}, of the bank has the form:

$$C^{Lr} = \frac{267.5}{300.25} = 0.89 < 1 \tag{2.5}$$

As the LCR < 1, the bank has to adjust its BS to become Basel III compliant.

2.2.2 Net Stable Funding Ratio

The NSFR is determined by dividing the amount of available stable funding (ASF) by required stable funding (RSF) over a one-year stress period.[29] In the main, the NSFR strives to reduce the maturity mismatch between assets and liabilities with remaining contractual maturities of 1 year or more.[30]

2.2.2.1 Description of the NSFR

The description of the NSFR follows directly from several Basel documents on liquidity that are quoted in the text. During a stress scenario, stable funding the capital, and liability financing expected from reliable sources. In order to reduce the dependence on Central Banks, funding provided by them are excluded from NSFR liquidity standard evaluation.[31] The NSFR can be expressed as

$$NSFR = \frac{\text{Available Stable Funding}(ASF)}{\text{Required Stable Funding}(RSF)}. \tag{2.6}$$

Basel III requires that this ratio should be greater than one to ensure that the available funding meets the required funding over the evaluation period.[32] According to Basel III documentation, ASF is defined as the total amount of bank capital, preferred stock with maturity ≥ 1 year, liabilities with effective maturities ≥ 1 year, demand deposits or term deposits, or both, with maturities < 1 year, as well as wholesale funding with maturities < 1 year.[33,34] To calculate the actual ASF, the aforementioned capital and liability types have to be multiplied by a specific ASF factor assigned to each type. In the ASF calculation, capital, liabilities, and hybrids with a residual maturity of more than 1 year have a 100% weight, whereas stable deposits and less stable deposits are weighted by 90% and 80%, respectively. Wholesale funding from nonfinancials is weighted by 50%, whereas other wholesale funding is not recognized as stable funding.[35]

On the other hand, RSF is the weighted sum of the value of assets held and funded by the bank multiplied by a specific RSF factor assigned to each particular asset type. These weights can be more or less associated with the run-off rates in the LCR: Cash, commercial paper, bonds with a maturity of below 1 year, and nonrenewable interbank loans receive a weight of 0, whereas government bonds (including guaranteed debt from public sector entities, multilateral development banks, the European Commission (EC), Bank for International Settlements (BIS), and Central Banks as well as government) with a 0% risk weight under Basel II are assigned a weight of 5%.[36,37] Corporate and covered bonds with a rating of AA- or better with a residual maturity of 1 year or more have a 20% weight; whereas such bonds with a rating of below AA or at least A and a residual maturity of at least 1 year as well as loans to nonfinancial corporates with a residual maturity less than 1 year are assigned a 50% weight. Moreover, unencumbered mortgages with a risk-weight of up to 35% under Basel I receive a 65% RSF weight; retail loans with a residual maturity of less than 1 year get a 85% weight, whereas the rest receive a 100% weight.[38]

2.2.2.2 Implementation of the NSFR

In 2012, the observation period for considering amendments to the Basel III formulation of the NSFR announced in 2010 began. Originally the implementation of the NSFR was scheduled for Monday, January 1, 2018. However, because of experiences with the LCR, its implementation is likely to be delayed and, in an extreme case, could even be cancelled. Our results in Chapter 3 on the NSFR of big banks provide an insight into why this may happen.

2.2.2.3 Illustrative Example of the NSFR

By way of illustration, we compute the NSFR for Bank B that holds cash, government bonds, and retail loans. Bank B funds itself using a combination of stable and less stable deposits, unsecured wholesale funding (nonfinancial corporate), and equity. Table 2.4 presents the BS item values for our example.

The ASF, F^{AS}, depends on the ASF factors specified in the NSFR rules for liabilities. Denoting the ASF factor for liabilities of type j by Φ^j, it follows that:

$$F^{AS} = \Phi^{D^S} D^S + \Phi^{D^L} D^L + \Phi^{F^U} F^U + \Phi^E E \tag{2.7}$$
$$= 0.85 \times 150 + 0.70 \times 150 + 0.50 \times 210 + 1 \times 65 = 402.5,$$

where the ASF factors for stable retail deposits, less stable retail deposits, unsecured wholesale funding, and equity are 85%, 70%, 50%, and 100%, respectively.

The value of the RSF, F^{RS}, depends on the factors given in the NSFR specifications for various types of assets. Using Ψ^j to denote the RSF factor for type j liabilities, we have:

$$F^{RS} = \Psi^C C + \Psi^{BG} B^G + \Psi^\Lambda \Lambda \tag{2.8}$$
$$= 0.0 \times 50 + 0.05 \times 100 + 0.85 \times 425 = 366.25,$$

Table 2.4 Illustrative balance sheet for computing NSFR

Assets		Liabilities	
Cash (C)	50	Stable Retail Deposits (D^S)	150
Government Bonds (B^G)	100	Less Stable Retail Deposits (D^L)	150
Retail Loans (Λ)	425	Unsecured Wholesale Funding (F^U)	210
		Equity (E)	65
Total	575	Total	575

where the RSF factors for cash, government bonds, and retail loans are 0%, 5%, and 85%, respectively. Hence, the NSFR, F^{NSr}, of the bank can be computed as

$$F^{NSr} = \frac{402.5}{366.25} = 1.1 > 1.$$

Here, the NSFR exceeds 1, so Bank B complies with the new liquidity standard.

2.2.3 Traditional Liquidity Risk Measures

Besides the Basel III liquidity standards, LCR and NSFR, we also investigate traditional liquidity risk measures such as the NPAR, ROA, LIBOR-OISS, BIITKR, GSR, and BDR.

First, we consider the NPAR, where nonperforming assets are assets that are in jeopardy of default. Once the borrower has failed to make interest or principal payments for 90 days the asset is considered to be nonperforming. Moreover, the NPAR is the ratio of nonperforming assets to effective capital, where such capital is constituted by tangible common equity and loan and lease loss reserves. The predictive power of bank failure of the NPAR (compared to the Texas ratio) is robust and reliable.[39]

Second, return-on-assets (ROA), is the ratio of the net income to total assets and is an indicator of how profitable a firm is relative to its total assets. In other words, the profitability measure, ROA, is an indication of a bank's ability to generate a positive net income from its asset investments. The existing literature suggests that as the ROA increases, bank liquidity will rise commensurately. ROA gives an idea as to how efficient management is at using its assets to generate earnings.

For a specified loan term, LIBOR is the rate at which banks are willing to lend to other banks. The OIS rate is the rate on a derivative contract on the overnight rate. In the United States, the overnight rate corresponds to the effective federal funds rate. Here, over the term of the contract, two parties agree that one will pay the other an interest rate that is the difference between the term OIS rate and the geometric average of the overnight federal funds rate. The OIS rate is a measure of the market's expectation of the overnight funds rate over the contract term. The OIS market is almost devoid of default risk because there is no exchange of principal. Funds are only exchanged at the maturity of the contract, when one party pays the net interest obligation to the other. The LIBOR-OISS is assumed to be a measure of bank prosperity because it reflects what banks believe is the risk of default associated with lending to other banks. In essence, it is a measure of market-wide liquidity risk.[40]

The Basel II total capital ratio (BIITKR) is the bank's total capital to assets ratio. The BIITKR is adequately characterized in the BCBS documents.[41,42] The government securities ratio (GSR) is the ratio of government securities to effective capital. Brokered deposits is a large-denomination bank deposit that is sold by a bank to a brokerage, which then divides it into smaller pieces for sale to its customers. Core deposits—such as deposits to checking accounts, savings accounts and certificates of deposit made by individuals—are the other key component of a bank's deposits. The brokered deposits ratio (BDR) is the ratio of brokered deposits to total assets. The GSR (proxy for asset liquidity) and BDR (proxy for fund stability) are comprehensively studied by Cullen.[43] Here, we note that liquidity risk measures for asset liquidity include the GSR and LCR whereas funding stability is measured by the BDR and NSFR.

2.3 Preliminaries on Basel III, Liquidity Creation and Bank Capital

Liquidity creation is related to the ability of banks to extend loans of limited liquidity to borrowers while providing demand depositors with the opportunity to withdraw funds at par value. In Chapter 4, we analyze causality and its directionality for bank *capital* and *liquidity creation* (broad and narrow measure) in large, medium, and small banks. To achieve this, we adopt the Granger causality approach. Secondly, we investigate liquidity creation and the banking risks associated with it. In a Basel III context, these risks can be associated with earnings volatility, credit, and nonperforming loans. Moreover, as control variables, we include size, market share, inflation, and unemployment. Here, we show

how Basel III capital and liquidity requirements may be employed to manage these risks.

We agree with Berger and Bouwman[44] that at least two hypotheses describe the relationship between bank capital and liquidity creation. The first is the "financial fragility/crowding-out" hypothesis and the other is the "risk absorption" hypothesis. According to the former, higher capital is associated with less monitoring which leads to less liquidity creation.[45,46] On the other hand, the risk absorption hypothesis forecasts that higher capital facilitates the banks' ability to create liquidity. This hypothesis evolved from two elements of literature, highlighting the role of banks as risk transformers. Whereas banks' exposure to risk is elevated by liquidity creation,[47,48] capital allows banks to absorb greater risk.[49,50] In principle, higher capital enhances the ability of banks to create liquidity because it allows them to absorb greater risk.[51,52]

2.4 Preliminaries on Basel III, Liquidity Regulation and the Economy

Liquidity risk originated from both BS and OBS sources during the financial crisis of 2007 through 2009. As far as the former is concerned, banks that had a major reliance on deposit and equity financing, that is, stable funding sources, continued to extend credit to other banks. Banks that held more illiquid BS assets, by contrast, increased asset liquidity and reduced lending. On the other hand, OBS liquidity risk materialized on the BS and compelled new credit extension as increased takedown demand displaced lending capacity. In general, efforts by banks to manage the liquidity crisis led to a decline in credit supply.[53]

Chapter 5 emphasizes that during the 2007 to 2009 financial crisis, banks received cash demands from counterparties, short-term creditors, and existing borrowers. Credit extension decreased, with banks that were hit hardest by liquidity pressures being most severely constrained. Central bank emergency lending programs were implemented to mitigate the resulting risk.[54,55] Currently, liquidity risks originate more from exposure to idiosyncratic interbank lending and borrowing practices rather than deposit outflows. The former arise from fund withdrawals from wholesale short-term financing arrangements, unused loan commitments, derivatives markets margin calls, and obligations to repurchase (repos) securitized assets. For instance, banks extend credit lines that make credit available on demand as well as extend loan commitments of various types. Greater use of such commitments increased risk. When liquidity decreased, more borrowers availed themselves of existing credit line funds. For example, during the 2007 to 2009 financial crisis, when the commercial paper market imploded, short-term funds were not readily available to nonfinancial institutions. As obligations became due, the issuers of such paper alternatively utilized previously arranged backup lines at banks to refinance their paper. Banks were compelled to extend such credit with the result that the new credit extension suffered.[56,57]

It is anticipated that the Basel III liquidity regulation will affect the macroeconomy via an increase in bank intermediation costs. More specifically, under the new regulation, banks must hold more capital, that is, they must deleverage. If the required return on equity and cost of bank debt do not adjust, then banks will increase lending spreads to compensate for the higher cost of funding. In this way, Basel III liquidity regulation will badly affect sovereign credit as well as macroeconomic variables such as GDP, investment, inflation, consumption, personal disposable income, personal savings, and employment (H. Depp, personal communication, March–July 2013).

CHAPTER 3

Basel III Liquidity Regulation and Bank Failure

In the Basel III Accord, liquidity risk is measured via the liquidity coverage ratio (LCR) and net stable funding ratio (NSFR). In this chapter, we estimate the LCR and NSFR by applying approximation techniques to banking data from a cross section of countries. We find that these Basel III risk measures have low information values and are relatively poor indicators of liquidity risk.[1]

Our results, in this chapter, show that as the LCR increases or decreases the probability of failure decreases or increases for both Class I (internationally active banks with Basel III Tier 1 capital (BIIIT1K) in excess of $4 billion) and Class II (the rest) banks. The same is true for the NSFR of Class II banks. However, the anomaly is that Class I bank failure probability is positively correlated with NSFR. This is a clear indication that at this point NSFR regulation still has to be refined before its envisaged implementation on Monday, January 1, 2018.

Furthermore, we show how liquidity affects bank insolvency and failure. We also establish that market-wide liquidity risk, proxied by LIBOR-OISS, was a major predictor of bank failures in 2009 and 2010, whereas idiosyncratic liquidity risk, proxied by other liquidity risk measures, was less so.[2]

3.1 Background to Basel III Liquidity Regulation and Bank Failure

In this section, we provide a terse review of salient features of Basel III liquidity regulation and bank failure.

3.1.1 Review of Basel III Liquidity Regulation and Bank Failure

The LCR aims to create a mechanism whereby liquidity problems over a 30-day horizon can be combated.[3] Maintenance of a minimum for the aforementioned standard aims to ensure that banks have appropriate amounts of unencumbered high-quality liquid assets (HQLAs) to counteract the net cash outflows it experiences during acute short-term stress scenarios.[4-6] These scenarios mimic conditions experienced in the 2007 to 2009 financial crisis with respect to institution-specific and systemic shocks.[7] By contrast, the NSFR limits the over-reliance on short-term wholesale funding during market liquidity buoyancy and encourages improved assessment of liquidity risk for on-balance sheet (BS) and off-balance sheet (OBS) items.

In this chapter, we also ascertain how Economic Modeling and Econometric Research Group (EMERG) global results for LCR and NSFR compare with those of the Basel Committee on Banking Supervision (BCBS)[8-12] and European Banking Authority (EBA).[13-16]

Existing literature suggests that imposing higher liquidity standards makes it less likely that banks will compromise their solvency and engage in excessive credit extension.[17] This should protect banks against systemic risks and consequent financial crises.[18] The paper BCBS262 finds incentives to hold a greater stock of HQLAs.[19,20] Our analysis supports this claim in the case of the LCR of Class I and II banks.

Distinguin et al. claims that banks build bigger capital buffers when they are exposed to higher illiquidity.[21] Furthermore, Garleanu and Pedersen show that tighter risk management of individual banks, as proposed by Basel III, could lead to market illiquidity at the aggregate level.[22] Our contribution also investigates this assertion by assessing the effectiveness of Basel III liquidity measures in terms of increasing bank liquidity and decreasing failures.[23-26]

With regard to methodology, our analysis is most similar to that of Wu and Hong[27,28] as well as Hong, Huang, and Wu.[29] In their contributions, approximate measures of the Basel III LCR and NSFR are calculated using U.S. banking data. In particular, they studied a sample of U.S. banks covered by the Federal Deposit Insurance Corporation (FDIC) while ours was global and more heterogeneous (from various jurisdictions). For instance, we included the bank categories Class I and II in 38 countries. The study period in our paper was from 2002 to 2012 to include the 2007 through 2009 financial crisis, promulgation dates of Basel II and III as well as the quarter immediately prior to the implementation of the latter accord. Wu and Hong did not include 2012 data at all (ending in 2011) and could therefore not effectively study the period prior to the implementation of Basel III on Tuesday, 1 January 2013. Secondly, like us, they compare the information values of Basel III and traditional liquidity risk measures with regard to their predictive power for bank failures.[30] Also, Wu and Hong[31] estimate a discrete-time hazard model that distinguishes between idiosyncratic and market-wide liquidity risks.[32] Moreover, Hong, Huang, and Wu[33] find that the probability of failure of U.S. commercial banks is negatively correlated with the NSFR, whereas it is positively correlated with the LCR. They conclude that this connection between bank failure and LCR highlights the negative externality of liquidity hoarding. Our results differ from theirs in these respects. Thirdly, we note that U.S. banks did not officially adopt Basel II capital regulation. Unlike Wu and Hong, we insisted that all the banks in our sample be Basel II compliant. In our opinion, our conclusions were different from theirs in several respects. However, we attributed conclusions that did not differ dramatically, to the standard assumptions about the data, the relatively high proportion of U.S. banking data used by us and the similarity in the methodology. However, in general, the latter can be considered to be standard for bank failure analysis. In this respect, our results on the connection between bank failure and Basel III liquidity standards differ on most accounts from Wu and Hong[34,35] as well as Hong, Huang, and Wu.[36]

The current chapter has strong connections with the aforementioned contributions in that, for Class I and II banks, we investigate how bank failures and liquidity risk are related. Except for Wu and Hong[37,38] (see, also, Hong, Huang, and Wu[39]), our methodology differs from the aforementioned outputs because we employ a technique that involves the estimation of discrete-time hazard models. Also, our contribution analyzes the notion of liquidity risk even further than before by determining whether market-wide liquidity risk (via the LIBOR-OISS) was the major contributor to Class I and II bank failures during the 2007 to 2009 financial crisis. Our study also incorporates the latest Basel III prescripts that were published in 2013.

3.1.2 Basel III Liquidity Regulation and Bank Failure Data

We consider EMERG global liquidity data that consists of observations for a wide cross section of banks for the period 2002 through 2012.[40] In particular; we use data from the income statements of individual banks as well as information about BS and OBS items.

3.1.2.1 Class I and II Banks

We investigate liquidity for Class I banks that hold more than $4 billion in BIIIT1K and are internationally active. Moreover, we consider Class II banks that violate one or both of these conditions.[41] In reality, some Class II banks considered could have been classified as Class I if they were internationally active. Nevertheless, these banks make a large contribution to the total assets of Class II banks. Invariably, all Class I banks can also be classified as large in that their gross total assets (GTA) exceed $3 billion (see Chapter 4 for further discussion on large banks). Many of the banks in our study come from jurisdictions affiliated to the BCBS and Macro-Economic Assessment Group (MAG).

Our investigation includes 157 Class I and 234 Class II LIBOR-based banks from 38 countries. These banks (with the number of Class I and Class II banks in parenthesis for each jurisdiction, as well as * and 'denoting BCBS and MAG members, respectively) are located in Argentina* (1,3), Australia*' (5,2), Austria (2,5), Belgium* (1,2), Botswana (1,1), Brazil*' (3,1), Canada*' (7,3), China*' (7,1), Czech Republic (4,3), Finland (0,14), France*' (5,5), Germany*' (7,24), Hong Kong SAR* (1,8), Hungary (1,2), India* (6,6), Indonesia* (1,3), Ireland (3,1), Italy*' (2,11), Japan*' (14,5), Korea*' (6,4), Luxembourg* (0,1), Malta (0,3), Mexico*' (1,8), Namibia (0,1), the Netherlands*' (3,13), Norway (1,6), Poland (0,5), Portugal (3,3), Russia* (0,3), Saudi Arabia*

(4,1), Singapore* (5,0), South Africa* (4,5), Spain*' (2,4), Sweden* (4,0), Switzerland*' (3,5), Turkey* (7,1), United Kingdom*' (8,5) and United States*' (35,66). In order to limit depositor losses, all 38 jurisdictions have explicit deposit insurance schemes or implicit government protection schemes for banks.

3.1.2.2 Basel III Liquidity Regulation and Bank Failure
Data Restrictions

In our study, we did not consider Central Banks, subsidiaries, banks with incomplete (inconsistent or noncontinuous) information nor observations with negative HQLA, net cash outflow (NCO), available stable funding (ASF), required stable funding (RSF), or other values.[42,43] Furthermore, we use nonpermanent samples that do not suffer from survivorship bias to study cross sectional patterns. For our sample, bank failure data for the period 2002 through 2012 was obtained from deposit insurance schemes or implicit government protection schemes. For instance, for the United States, such data was obtained from the Federal Deposit Insurance Corporation (FDIC).[44,45] We choose the period 2002 to 2012 because available EMERG global liquidity data does not allow us to reliably determine the LCR and NSFR prior to 2002.[46]

Where insufficient data existed, we determined a first best approximation or omitted the liquidity parameter completely. In the latter, the aggregate data obtained was adjusted accordingly.

3.1.2.3 Basel III Liquidity Regulation and Bank Failure
Data Computations

Estimating the LCR and NSFR using available EMERG public data proved to be a challenge. Firstly, the prescripts for these risk standards are sometimes ambiguous and subject to frequent regulatory amendment. For instance, the final rules relating to the LCR were only published on Monday, January 7, 2013.[47]

Secondly, the EMERG global banking data has several limitations in terms of granularity and format when compared with the information required to determine the Basel III liquidity standards.[48] In all instances, we had to make difficult choices when applying Basel III guidelines to such a large diversity of banks.

We compute the LCR from the amendments introduced on Monday, 7 January 2013(ADD Reference Basel Committee on Banking Supervision (BCBS). (2013, January). *Basel III: The liquidity coverage ratio and liquidity risk monitoring tools.*Bank for International Settlements (BIS) Publications.Retrieved June 25, 2013, from http://www.bis.org/publ/bcbs238.htm). The method of computing the LCR, released by the BCBS on this date, include an expansion in the range of assets eligible as HQLA and some refinements to the assumed inflow and outflow rates to more accurately reflect conditions in times of stress.

3.1.3 Chapter 3: Main Contributions

The responses to the questions posed in the following list provide the main contributions made in this chapter about Basel III liquidity regulation[49] and bank failure:

- **Question 3.1.1 (Approximations of Basel III and Traditional Liquidity Risk Measures).** *How can we approximate the Basel III and traditional liquidity risk measures for Class I and II banks? (see Subsection 3.2.1).*
- **Question 3.1.2 (Key Statistics of Liquidity Risk Measures)** *For Class I and II banks, what are the most important features of the key statistics related to Basel III and traditional liquidity risk measures ? (see Subsection 3.2.2).*
- **Question 3.1.3 (LCR and NSFR Shortfalls)** *What is the impact of LCR and NSFR shortfalls for Class I and II banks ? (see Subsection 3.2.3).*
- **Question 3.1.4 (Comparison with BCBS and EBA Results)** *How do our results for LCR and NSFR compare with those of the BCBS and EBA ? (see Subsection 3.2.4).*

- **Question 3.1.5 (Information Values for Liquidity Risk Measures)** *For Class I and II banks, how sensitive are Basel III liquidity risk measures by comparison to traditional ones ? In particular, how do LCR and NSFR information values compare with those of traditional risk measures (in particular, NPAR, ROA, LIBOR-OISS, BIITKR, GSR and BDR) for Class I and II banks ? (see Subsection 3.3.1).*

- **Question 3.1.6 (Bank Failure Rates)** *For Class I and II banks, what are the bank failure rates for the period 2002 to 2012 ? (see Subsection 3.3.2).*

- **Question 3.1.7 (Estimating Discrete-Time Hazard Models)** *How can discrete-time hazard models for Class I and II banks be estimated and used to characterize their failure ? (see Subsection 3.3.3).*

- **Question 3.1.8 (Contribution of Liquidity Risk to Bank Failure)** *How can we ascertain whether idiosyncratic or market-wide liquidity risk was the major contributor to Class I and II bank failures during the 2007 to 2009 financial crisis ? (see Subsections 3.3.3 and 3.3.4).*

- **Question 3.1.9 (Policy Implications for Basel III Liquidity Regulation and Bank Failure)** *What are some of the policy implications for Basel III liquidity regulation as it relates to Class I and II bank failure ? (see Section 3.4).*

3.2 Basel III and Traditional Liquidity Risk Measures

In this section, we discuss Basel III and traditional liquidity risk measures for both Class I and II banks.

3.2.1 Approximate Measures of Basel III and Traditional Liquidity Risk Measures

In this subsection, we first approximate values for the Basel III liquidity risk measures, namely, LCR[50] and NSFR. The following figures provide plots of the liquidity risk measures as well as traditional ones.

Next, Figure 3.1 displays approximate values for the LCR, NSFR, GSR, and BDR of Class I and II banks.

Figure 3.1 shows that LCR and NSFR for both Class I and II banks had been in a downward trend from 02Q4 until 07Q3. It is interesting that throughout the 2002 to 2012 period, a greater disparity existed between the NSFR for Class I and II banks than for the LCR of the same types of banks. The average LCR and NSFR had increased dramatically subsequent to the onset of the 2007 to 2009 financial crisis. This trend persisted for the LCR immediately before and after the announcement of Basel III liquidity regulation. On the other hand, the average NSFR had risen sharply from 07Q3 to 10Q1 for Class II banks. The upward trend for the NSFR for Class I banks persisted until the end of the financial crisis reaching a higher peak than any of the other Basel III liquidity risk measures. This unexpected phenomenon makes the Class I NSFR a very interesting topic of discussion.

Also from Figure 3.1, for both Class I and II banks, we conclude that the GSR declined until 2008, with the trend reversing thereafter. On the other hand, the average BDR had been in an upward trend from 2001 through 2008, followed by a trend reversal. The BDR for Class II banks exceeds those of Class I banks from 11Q4 onward.

Analogous to Figure 3.1, we can represent NPAR, ROA, LIBOR-OISS, and BIITKR for Class I and II banks as follows.

Figure 3.2 shows that the NPAR for Class I and II banks rose sharply from 07Q3 to 09Q3 when it peaked. On the other hand, the average ROA decreased dramatically during the 2007 through 2009 financial crisis reaching negative territory at the end of the crisis. A drastic recovery in terms of profitability can be discerned after this period although ROA never reached the levels that it was at prior to the financial crisis again. The LIBOR-OISS remained flat from 03Q1 until 07Q3, after which there was a sizeable increase in this spread that peaked in 08Q3. This was followed by a sharp decrease in LIBOR-OISS till the end of the crisis. Relative stability followed this trend. On the other hand, for Class I banks, the BIITKR steadily increased until 10Q3, after which there was a sudden decrease in this capital ratio. For Class II banks, from 03Q1 till

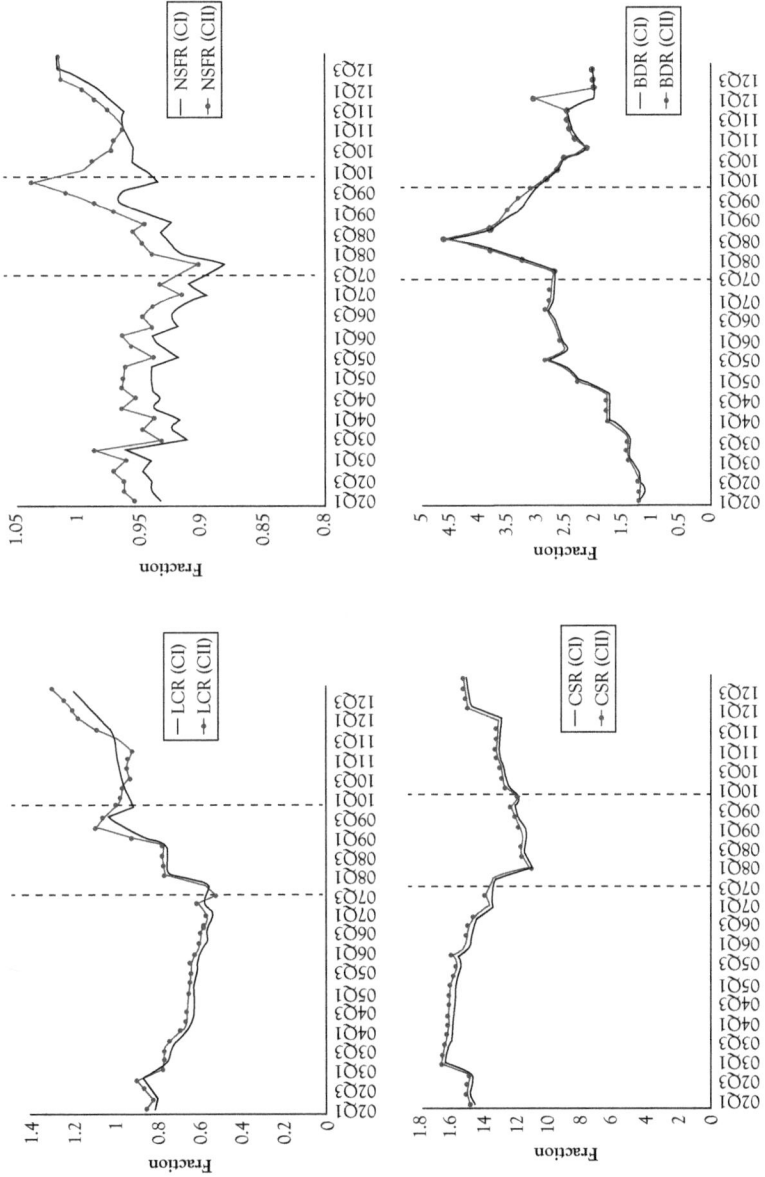

Figure 3.1 LCR, NSFR, GSR, and BDR for Class I and II banks

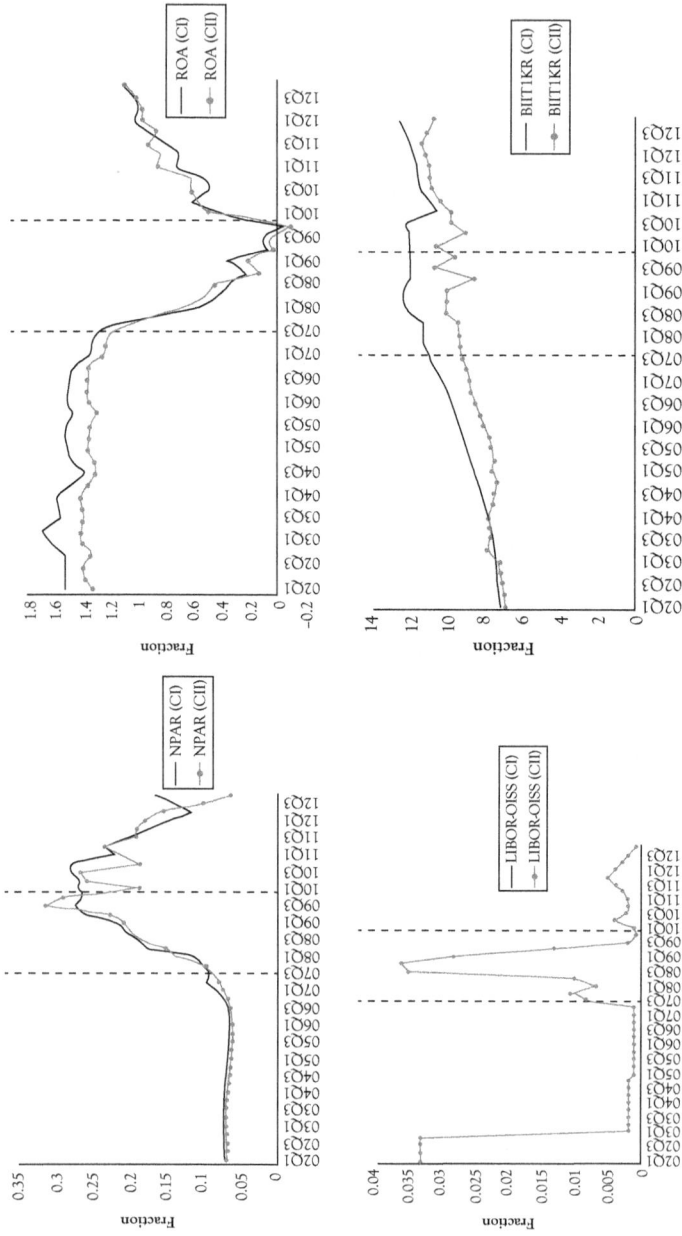

Figure 3.2 NPAR, ROA, LIBOR-OISS, and BIITKR for Class I and II banks

12Q4, the BIITKR was significantly lower and more volatile than for their Class I counterparts.

3.2.2 Descriptive Statistics of Liquidity Risk Measures

In Table 3.1, the mean, median, standard deviation, skewness, kurtosis, and Jarque Bera statistics for LCR, NSFR, GSR, and BDR are provided.

The means and medians of the LCR for both Class I and II banks are much lower than that of the NSFR. However, the NSFR has a much lower standard deviation.

In Table 3.2, the mean, median, standard deviation, skewness, kurtosis, and Jarque Bera statistics for NPAR, ROA, LIBOR-OISS, and BIITKR are described.

3.2.3 LCR and NSFR Shortfalls

In order to satisfy Basel III LCR standards and negate shortfalls, banks can reduce risky business activities during a short-term liquidity shock or lengthen the funding term beyond 30 days.[51] Banks may also increase

Table 3.1 Descriptive statistics of LCR, NSFR, GSR, and BDR for Class I and II Banks

Parameter	Basel III liquidity standards LCR/NSFR		Traditional liquidity risk measures GSR/BDR	
Mean	(0.793,0.817)	(0.942,0.964)	(0.142,0.144)	(0.024,0.024)
Median	(0.749,0.774)	(0.940,0.963)	(0.149,0.151)	(0.024,0.025)
Maximum	(1.193,1.290)	(1.017,1.036)	(0.166,0.168)	(0.044,0.045)
Minimum	(0.540,0.514)	(0.880,0.901)	(0.112,0.114)	(0.011,0.011)
Std. Dev.	(0.190,0.203)	(0.029,0.028)	(0.016,0.016)	(0.008,0.008)
Skewness	(0.361,0.544)	(0.568,0.343)	(−0.248,−0.242)	(0.334,0.305)
Kurtosis	(1.945,2.390)	(3.700,3.132)	(1.782,1.782)	(2.847,2.833)
Jarque-Bera	(2.996,2.851)	(3.268,0.895)	(3.171,3.148)	(0.861,0.732)
Probability	(0.224,0.240)	(0.195,0.639)	(0.205,0.207)	(0.650,0.693)
Sum	(34.908,35.944)	(41.438,42.414)	(6.254,6.337)	(1.045,1.062)
Sum Sq. Dev	(1.544,1.775)	(0.035,0.034)	(0.011,0.011)	(0.002,0.003)
Observations	(44,44)	(44,44)	(44,44)	(44,44)

Table 3.2 Descriptive statistics of NPAR, ROA, LIBOR-OISS, and BIITKR for Class I and II banks

Parameter	Basel III liquidity standards NPAR/ROA		Traditional liquidity risk measures LIBOR-OISS/ BIITKR	
Mean	(0.133,0.125)	(1.058,0.989)	(0.005,0.005)	(0.120,0.110)
Median	(0.093,0.075)	(1.295,1.205)	(0.002,0.002)	(0.119,0.109)
Maximum	(0.279,0.311)	(1.690,1.410)	(0.036,0.036)	(0.133,0.116)
Minimum	(0.062,0.059)	(−0.040,−0.090)	(0.001,0.001)	(0.113,0.105)
Std. Dev.	(0.078,0.075)	(0.519,0.447)	(0.008,0.008)	(0.004,0.004)
Skewness	(0.713,0.822)	(−0.601,−0.939)	(2.949,2.949)	(0.967,0.608)
Kurtosis	(1.927,2.345)	(1.944,2.676)	(10.782,10.782)	(3.210,2.049)
Jarque-Bera	(5.843,5.749)	(4.698,6.661)	(174.827,174.827)	(6.941,4.365)
Probability	(0.053,0.056)	(0.095,0.035)	(0.000,0.000)	(0.031,0.113)
Sum	(5.889,5.541)	(46.580,43.540)	(0.221,0.221)	(5.258,4.815)
Sum Sq. Dev	(0.264,0.246)	(11.603,8.607)	(0.003,0.003)	(0.009,0.001)
Observations	(44,44)	(44,44)	(44,44)	(44,44)

their holdings of HQLAs. The Group of Central Bank Governors and Heads of Supervision (GHOS) agreed that, during stress scenarios, banks could use their existing HQLAs and thereby fall below the minimum. Moreover, it is the responsibility of bank supervisors to give guidance on how assets may be allocated under different circumstances.

3.2.3.1 LCR and NSFR Shortfalls for Class I and II Banks

Next, we report the LCR and NSFR shortfalls for Class I and II banks.

From Figure 3.3, for Class I and II banks, the general trend is for LCR and NSFR shortfalls to decrease in the 2002 to 2012 period. This tendency is more pronounced for the LCR than the NSFR. An interesting feature of the shortfalls is that they were both rather flat for a large part of the 2007 through 2009 financial crisis. However, the NSFR shortfall for Class I was particularly volatile toward the end of the crisis. The LCR has reacted more strongly to the announcement of the Basel III liquidity standards than the NSFR. This must be seen in the light of the fact that LCR regulation has already been finalized[52] with the LCR set to be implemented on Thursday, January 1, 2015, whereas the NSFR will be implemented much later on Monday, January 1, 2018.

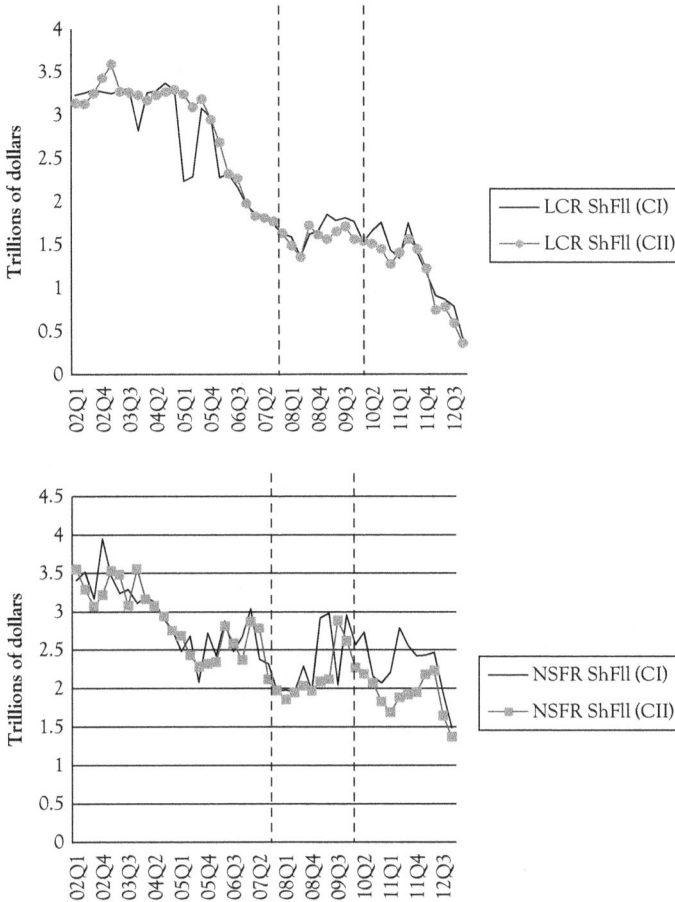

Figure 3.3 LCR and NSFR shortfalls for Class I and II banks

3.2.3.2 Case Study: South African LCR and NSFR Shortfalls

In this subsection, we determine the LCR and NSFR shortfalls in the South African (SA) banking industry. Due to the dependence on cost, various factors are considered in order to provide an accurate assessment of the shortfalls in these Basel III liquidity standards at the end of 12Q4 (H. Depp, personal communication, March–July 2013).

For the LCR shortfall, we consider that (a) the HQLA's carry cost, (b) the historical range of the HQLAs, and (c) in the absence of HQLA holdings, we assume that alternative measures to reduce the LCR would be at a similar cost. This is because the HQLA carry cost is an opportunity cost (H. Depp, personal communication, March–July 2013).

For the NSFR shortfall, we consider (a) increases in the retail fund cost across the funding base; (b) for the stable funding gap, we assume that 20% is funded offshore at spreads of 100 to 125 bps above the offshore bond issuance by SA, and (c) we suppose that the balance of the stable funding shortfall is funded in the domestic capital market. Also, we assume that funding spreads are higher than those in 12Q4 due to the dramatic increase in credit extension by SA banks subsequent to the financial crisis (H. Depp, personal communication, March–July 2013).

Given the aforementioned factors, we can determine the LCR and NSFR shortfalls for the SA banking sector. At the end of 12Q4, the estimated gross shortfall was $14 billion and $45 billion for the LCR and NSFR, respectively. A rough approximation (72 bps) of the implied impact on the borrowing cost to close these gaps is 8.7 bps for the LCR and 62.8 bps for the NSFR.

3.2.4 Comparison with BCBS and EBA Results

Some of the first quantitative studies on Basel III liquidity standards are reported in Basel documents[53–57] and EBA papers.[58–61] Summary tables of these contributions are presented as follows.

Table 3.3 is constituted by 2010 and 2012 Basel documents[62–64] and EBA papers.[65,66]

Table 3.4 is constituted by 2013 Basel documents[67,68] and EBA papers.[69,70]

3.3 Liquidity Risk, Insolvency, and Bank Failure

In this section, we present the results on the relationship between Basel III and traditional liquidity risk measures and bank failure for Class I and II banks.

3.3.1 Liquidity Risk Measure Sensitivity for Class I and II Banks

In this subsection, for Class I and II banks, we distinguish the sensitivity of the approximate Basel III liquidity risk measures from traditional ones. In our context, a risk measure is considered to be more risk sensitive if it has higher power of predicting bank failures. In particular, we compare the power of different risk measures for predicting bank failures within 1 year.[71,72]

In a manner similar to Hong, Huang, and Wu,[73] we divide the data of each variable into 10 deciles and calculate its information value for

Table 3.3 2009 and 2011 BCBS and EBA liquidity studies

Organization Contribution Report Date Bank Data Date	BCBS			EBA	
	BCBS231 (Sep 2012) Sep-2012 12/31/2011	BCBS217 (Apr 2012) Apr-2012 06/30/2011	BCBS186 (Dec 2012) Dec-10 12/31/2009	EBA (Sep 2012) Sep-12 12/31/2011	EBA (Apr 2012) Apr-12 06/30/2011
Bank count	(102,107)	(103,102)	(94,169)	(44,112)	(48,110)
Total Assets (Euro Trillions)	47.40	45.18	41.3	31.00	31.00
Weighted Average LCR	(0.91,0.98)	(0.90,0.83)	(0.83,0.98)	(0.72,0.91)	(0.71,0.70)
LCR Shortfall (Euro Trillions)	1.83	1.76	1.73	1.17	1.15
Weighted Average NSFR	(0.98,0.95)	(0.94,0.93)	(0.93,1.03)	(0.93,0.94)	(0.89,0.90)
NSFR Shortfall (Euro Trillions)	2.50	2.80	2.89	1.4	1.93

Table 3.4 *2012 BCBS and EBA liquidity studies*

	BCBS			EBA		
Organization Contribution Report Date Bank Data Date	BCBS278 (Mar 2014) Mar-2014 06/30/2013	BCBS262 (Sep 2013) Sep-2013 12/31/2012	BCBS243 (Sep 2013) Apr-2013 06/30/2012	EBA (Mar 2014) Mar-2014 06/30/2013	EBA (Sep 2013) Sep-2013 12/31/2012	EBA (Apr 2013) Apr-2013 06/30/2012
Bank count	(102,125)	(102,107)	(101,108)	(43,131)	(42,128)	(44,113)
Total Assets (Euro Trillions)	62	63.10	45.18	31.7	31.00	31.50
Weighted Average LCR	(1.14,1.32)	(1.19,1.26)	(NC, NC)	(1.04,1.32)	(1.09,1.27)	(NC, NC)
LCR Shortfall (Euro Trillions)	0.536	0.563	NC	0.262	0.225	NC
Weighted Average NSFR	(NC, NC)	(1.00,0.99)	(0.99,1.00)	(NC, NC)	(0.96,0.96)	(0.94,0.99)
NSFR Shortfall (Euro Trillions)	(NC, NC)	2.00	2.40	(NC, NC)	0.959	1.2

NC – not computed

Table 3.5 Information values of liquidity risk measures for Class I and II banks

Rank	Liquidity risk measure	Information value: V^I
1.	NPAR	(0.64051,0.61531)
2.	ROA	(0.53527,0.56875)
3.	LIBOR-OISS	(0.50362,0.47648)
4.	BIITKR	(0.30604,0.32541)
5.	GSR	(0.16605,0.14979)
6.	BDR	(0.12814,0.11291)
7.	LCR	(0.08337,0.06974)
8.	NSFR	(0.03868,0.04962)

predicting bank failures.[74] Table 3.5 reports the information value of the eight liquidity risk measures, NPAR, ROA, LIBOR-OISS, BIITKR, GSR, BDR, LCR, and NSFR.

As Table 3.5 shows, for both Class I and II banks, the LCR and NSFR rank very low in terms of liquidity risk sensitivity by comparison to other risk measures. In this regard, LCR and NSFR information values—(0.08337, 0.06974) and (0.03868, 0.04962), respectively—are much lower than those of the six traditional liquidity risk measures under investigation.[75] The Class I bank liquidity risk measures, NPAR, LIBOR-OISS, GSR, BDR, and LCR have information values that are greater than those for their Class II counterparts.

3.3.2 Class I and II Bank Failure

The bank failure rates for the 391 banks from 38 countries in our sample for the period 2002 to 2012 are given in Table 3.6.

From Table 3.6, we note that 6 Class I and 17 Class II banks failed in the period 2002 to 2012. As we have seen before, both the LCR and NSFR have questionable power to discriminate on the basis of liquidity risk for Class I and II banks.[76,77] It is interesting to note that, in support of Basel III liquidity regulation, we found that higher LCRs are associated with lower subsequent bank failure rates. This finding is different from many studies[78,79] of the U.S. banking industry.

Table 3.7 provides the bank failure rate by decile for Class I and II banks in the case of the LCR, NSFR, and six other liquidity risk measures.

Table 3.6 Class I and Class II bank failures (2002–2012)

Quarter	Total bank count	Total bank failure	Bank failure rate	Class I and II bank count	Class I and II failures	Class I and II failure rate
02Q1	391	0	0.000	(157,234)	(0,0)	(0.000,0.000)
02Q2	391	1	0.003	(157,234)	(0,1)	(0.000,0.004)
02Q3	390	0	0.000	(157,233)	(0,0)	(0.000,0.000)
02Q4	390	0	0.000	(157,233)	(0,0)	(0.000,0.000)
03Q1	390	0	0.000	(157,233)	(0,0)	(0.000,0.000)
03Q2	390	0	0.000	(157,233)	(0,0)	(0.000,0.000)
03Q3	390	0	0.000	(157,233)	(0,0)	(0.000,0.000)
03Q4	390	0	0.000	(157,233)	(0,0)	(0.000,0.000)
04Q1	390	0	0.000	(157,233)	(0,0)	(0.000,0.000)
04Q2	390	0	0.000	(157,233)	(0,0)	(0.000,0.000)
04Q3	390	0	0.000	(157,233)	(0,0)	(0.000,0.000)
04Q4	390	0	0.000	(157,233)	(0,0)	(0.000,0.000)
05Q1	390	0	0.000	(157,233)	(0,0)	(0.000,0.000)
05Q2	390	0	0.000	(157,233)	(0,0)	(0.000,0.000)
05Q3	390	0	0.000	(157,233)	(0,0)	(0.000,0.000)
05Q4	390	0	0.000	(157,233)	(0,0)	(0.000,0.000)
06Q1	390	0	0.000	(157,233)	(0,0)	(0.000,0.000)
06Q2	390	0	0.000	(157,233)	(0,0)	(0.000,0.000)
06Q3	390	0	0.000	(157,233)	(0,0)	(0.000,0.000)
06Q4	390	0	0.000	(157,233)	(0,0)	(0.000,0.000)
07Q1	390	0	0.000	(157,233)	(0,0)	(0.000,0.000)
07Q2	390	0	0.000	(157,233)	(0,0)	(0.000,0.000)
07Q3	390	0	0.000	(157,233)	(0,0)	(0.000,0.000)
07Q4	390	0	0.000	(157,233)	(0,0)	(0.000,0.000)
08Q1	390	0	0.000	(157,233)	(0,0)	(0.000,0.000)
08Q2	390	0	0.000	(157,233)	(0,0)	(0.000,0.000)
08Q3	390	1	0.000	(157,233)	(0,1)	(0.000,0.000)
08Q4	389	2	0.003	(157,232)	(1,1)	(0.006,0.004)
09Q1	387	1	0.005	(156,231)	(0,1)	(0.000,0.004)
09Q2	386	2	0.003	(156,230)	(1,1)	(0.006,0.004)
09Q3	384	4	0.005	(155,229)	(1,3)	(0.006,0.013)
09Q4	380	4	0.010	(154,226)	(2,2)	(0.013,0.009)

Table 3.6 (Continued)

Quarter	Total bank count	Total bank failure	Bank failure rate	Class I and II bank count	Class I and II failures	Class I and II failure rate
10Q1	376	3	0.008	(152,224)	(1,2)	(0.007,0.009)
10Q2	373	2	0.005	(151,222)	(0,2)	(0.000,0.009)
10Q3	371	0	0.000	(151,220)	(0,0)	(0.000,0.000)
10Q4	371	0	0.000	(151,220)	(0,0)	(0.000,0.000)
11Q1	371	0	0.000	(151,220)	(0,0)	(0.000,0.000)
11Q2	371	1	0.003	(151,220)	(0,1)	(0.000,0.005)
11Q3	370	0	0.000	(151,219)	(0,0)	(0.000,0.000)
11Q4	370	0	0.000	(151,219)	(0,0)	(0.000,0.000)
12Q1	370	0	0.000	(151,219)	(0,0)	(0.000,0.000)
12Q2	370	1	0.003	(151,219)	(0,1)	(0.000,0.005)
12Q3	369	1	0.003	(151,218)	(0,1)	(0.000,0.005)
12Q4	368	0	0.000	(151,217)	(0,0)	(0.000,0.000)

3.3.3 Estimating Discrete-Time Hazard Models for Class I and II Banks

In this subsection, we estimate four discrete-time hazard models for Class I and II banks.[80,81] The first model is based on equation (3.1) in Section 3.6. This is the benchmark model and is called model A.[82] In model B, we exclude the LCR and NSFR from model A but keep the LIBOR-OISS. Therefore, we can estimate the contribution of the LCR and NSFR for predicting bank failures by comparing models B and A. For model C, we exclude the LIBOR-OISS from model A but keep the LCR and NSFR. Comparison of models A and C allows us to measure the contribution of market-wide liquidity risk. Finally, model D excludes idiosyncratic and market-wide liquidity risk measures (i.e., the LCR, NSFR, and LIBOR-OISS).[83,84]

The model statistics include the number of observations, N, Pseudo R2, AIC, BIC, Log Likelihood, AUC Statistic, HL Statistic, and HL *p*-Value.[85,86] The estimation results are reported in the following table.

As can be seen from Table 3.8, there are small differences in model statistics between models A and B.[87,88] On the other hand, there are

Table 3.7 Bank failure rate by decile for Class I and II banks

Decile	LCR	NSFR	GSR	BDR	BIITKR	NPAR	ROA
0	(0.0030, 0.0030)	(0.0070, 0.0070)	(0.0210, 0.0210)	(–,–)	(0.0435, 0.04435)	(0.0000, 0.0000)	(0.0470, 0.0470)
1	(0.0020, 0.0020)	(0.0070, 0.0070)	(0.0120, 0.0120)	(–,–)	(0.0025, 0.0025)	(0.0000, 0.0000)	(0.0015, 0.0015)
2	(0.0010, 0.0010)	(0.0070, 0.0070)	(0.0070, 0.0070)	(–,–)	(0.0015, 0.0015)	(0.0007, 0.0007)	(0.0005, 0.0005)
3	(0.0030, 0.0030)	(0.0090, 0.0090)	(0.0050, 0.0050)	(0.0015, 0.0015)	(0.0015, 0.0015)	(0.0005, 0.0005)	(0.0000, 0.0000)
4	(0.0020, 0.0020)	(0.0060, 0.0060)	(0.0040, 0.0040)	(–,–)	(0.0010, 0.0010)	(0.0000, 0.0000)	(0.0000, 0.0000)
5	(0.0030, 0.0030)	(0.0040, 0.0040)	(0.0030, 0.0030)	(–,–)	(0.0005, 0.0005)	(0.0007, 0.0007)	(0.0003, 0.0003)
6	(0.0040, 0.0040)	(0.0040, 0.0040)	(0.0020, 0.0020)	(0.0040, 0.0040)	(0.0010, 0.0010)	(0.0015, 0.0015)	(0.0001, 0.0001)
7	(0.0060, 0.0060)	(0.0030, 0.0030)	(0.0010, 0.0010)	(0.0060, 0.0060)	(0.0000, 0.0000)	(0.0010, 0.0010)	(0.0005, 0.0005)
8	(0.0080, 0.0080)	(0.0020, 0.0020)	(0.0010, 0.0010)	(0.0115, 0.0115)	(0.0000, 0.0000)	(0.0015, 0.0015)	(0.0003, 0.0003)
9	(0.0200, 0.0200)	(0.0010, 0.0010)	(0.0000, 0.0000)	(0.0240, 0.0240)	(0.0000, 0.0000)	(0.0465, 0.0465)	(0.0010, 0.0010)

Table 3.8 Models A to D estimation results for Class I and II banks

	Model A	Model B LCR and NSFR excluded	Model C LIBOR-OISS excluded	Model D liquidity risk excluded
Panel A: Model Statistics				
N	(2 978,4 413)	(2 978,4 413)	(2 978,4 413)	(2 978,4 413)
Pseudo R²	(0.638,0.641)	(0.638,0.634)	(0.619,0.621)	(0.611,0.610)
AIC	(1729.67,1735.18)	(1751.13,1760.73)	(1839.80,1840.36)	(1889.73,1892.56)
BIC	(1848.77,1854.96)	(1863.47,1860.96)	(1976.74,1909.93)	(1980.86,1997.73)
Log Likelihood	(−853.79,−855.57)	(−87.657,−86.956)	(−918.16,−914.43)	(−938.86,−940.04)
AUC Statistic	(0.9823,0.9821)	(0.9832,0.9829)	(0.9807,0.9809)	(0.9842,0.9839)
HL Statistic	(19.841,19.983)	(6.464,6.089)	(21.747,20.947)	(24.963,25.072)
HL P-Value	(0.011,0.011)	(0.632,0.627)	(0.007,0.007)	(0.002,0.002)
Panel B: Parameter Estimates				
α^0	(−0.0085***,−0.0517***)	(−0.0023***,−0.0019***)	(0.0521***,0.0290***)	(0.0002,0.0010)
	([0.003],[0.003])	([0.0011],[0.0013])	([0.0024],[0.0026])	([0.0013],[0.0011])
α^1	(0.1010***,0.0406***)	(0.0888***,0.0354***)	(0.1082***,0.0406***)	(−0.0834***,−0.0322***)
	([0.010],[0.011])	([0.009],[0.010])	([0.008],[0.009])	([0.0007],[0.0007])
α^2	(−0.0140,−0.0137)	(−0.0143***,−0.0165***)	(−0.0133,−0.0137)	(0.0134***,0.0144***)
	([0.0112],[0.0111])	([0.0087],[0.0086])	([0.0117],[0.0116])	([0.0097],[0.0096])
α^3	(0.0201, 0.0006)	(0.0218***,0.0109***)	(0.0179, 0.0005)	(−0.0205,−0.0116)
	([0.0218],[0.0221])	([0.0203],[0.0205])	([0.0216],[0.0219])	([0.0197],[0.0200])

(Continued)

Table 3.8 (Continued)

	Model A	Model B LCR and NSFR excluded	Model C LIBOR-OISS excluded	Model D liquidity risk excluded
α^4	(−0.0018,0.0137) ([0.0039],[0.0034])	(0.0043,−0.0029) ([0.0037],[0.0041])	(−0.0111, 0.0137) ([0.0053],[0.0056])	(0.0072,0.0124) ([0.0055],[0.0066])
α^5	(−0.1135***,0.0867***) ([0.0297],[0.0297])	(−0.0884,−0.8119) ([0.0285],[0.0286])	(−0.1367***,0.0912***) ([0.0274],[0.0273])	(0.1069***,0.9680***) ([0.0246],[0.0247])
α^6	(0.1183***,0.1762***) ([0.0250],[0.0251])	(0.1095***,0.9477***) ([0.0648],[0.0649])	(0.1157***, 0.1720***) ([0.0490],[0.0490])	(−0.1054***, −1.0600***) ([0.0526],[0.0529])
α^7	(−0.0097***,0.0185***) ([0.0010],[0.0010])	(−0.0139***, −0.0233***) ([0.0009],[0.0010])	(−0.0103***,−0.0115***) ([0.0009],[0.0009])	(0.0164***,0.0210***) ([0.0008],[0.0009])
α^8	(−0.0009***,−0.0116***) ([0.1362],[0.1698])	(−0.0010***,−0.0002***) ([0.1354],[0.1688])	(−0.0086, 0.0007) ([0.1535],[0.1914])	(0.0009,−0.0007) ([0.1566],[0.1952])
α^9	(−0.0001,0.0007) ([0.0006],[0.0004])	(−0.0002,−0.0006) ([0.0008],[0.0008])	(0.0002, −0.0000) ([0.0005],[0.0007]])	(0.0002,0.0001) ([0.0007],[0.0006])
α^{10}	(0.1042***,0.0031***) ([0.0091],[0.0092])	(0.1226***,0.1243***) ([0.0095],[0.0094])	(−,−) (−,−) ([-],[-])	(−,−) (−,−) ([-],[-])
α^{11}	(−0.0053, −0.0003) ([0.0286],[0.0293])	(−,−) ([-],[-])	(−0.0078,−0.0003) ([0.0250],[0.0266])	(−,−) ([-],[-])
α^{12}	(0.0111***,−0.0595***) ([0.0007],[0.0007])	(−,−) ([-],[-])	(0.0089***,−0.0600***) ([0.0008],[0.0008])	(−,−) ([-],[-])

substantial differences between model A and C that excludes the market-wide liquidity risk measures. Furthermore, the coefficient of LCR in model A is negative and insignificant, suggesting that the LCR has little bank failure predictive power. Our empirical results show that, in models A and C, the probability of failure is negatively correlated with the LCR for both Class I and II banks, while Class I bank failure probability is positively and Class II banks negatively correlated with the NSFR. However, the coefficient of the LIBOR-OISS is statistically significant and positive, which implies that market-wide liquidity risk is a significant predictor of bank failures. In the process of constituting Table 3.8, we can determine receiver operating characteristic (ROC) curves that measure rank-ordering power for models A through D. These ROC curves are similar, with model D having the highest AUC statistic.[89,90] This statistic is represented by the area under the ROC curves.

3.3.4 Observed and Predicted Bank Failure Rates for Class I and II Banks

Model A through D observed and predicted bank failure rates are displayed in the next table.

Table 3.9 provides information about the observed conditional failure rate and predicted values from models A to D.[91] Also, it displays the marginal contribution of the LCR and NSFR approximate measures for Class I and II banks. In addition, Table 3.9 presents the observed one-year conditional bank failure rates against the predicted values from models A to D. Columns 2, 3, and 4 display the observed one-year conditional bank failure rates against the predicted values from model A and B, which excludes the LCR and NSFR. The differences between the predictions of model A and B are negligible.[92,93] Since model B excludes the approximate measures of the LCR and NSFR, the differences between the predicted values of model A and B measure the marginal contribution of these approximate measures. As can be seen, the predicted failure rates of model A and B are very similar, and both closely match the observed failure rate for Class I and II banks.[94,95]

Table 3.9 Observed and predicted bank failure rates for Class I and II banks (2002–2012)

		Model A to D bank failures (2002–2012)			
	Observed bank failure rates	Predicted bank failure rates			
Quarter		Model A	Model B	Model C	Model D
02Q1	(0.000,0.000)	(0.000,0.000)	(0.000,0.000)	(0.000,0.000)	(0.000,0.000)
02Q2	(0.000,0.004)	(0.000,0.004)	(0.000,0.004)	(0.000,0.004)	(0.000,0.004)
02Q3	(0.000,0.000)	(0.000,0.000)	(0.000,0.000)	(0.000,0.000)	(0.000,0.000)
02Q4	(0.000,0.000)	(0.000,0.000)	(0.000,0.000)	(0.000,0.000)	(0.000,0.000)
03Q1	(0.000,0.000)	(0.000,0.000)	(0.000,0.000)	(0.000,0.000)	(0.000,0.000)
03Q2	(0.000,0.000)	(0.000,0.000)	(0.000,0.000)	(0.000,0.000)	(0.000,0.000)
03Q3	(0.000,0.000)	(0.000,0.000)	(0.000,0.000)	(0.000,0.000)	(0.000,0.000)
03Q4	(0.000,0.000)	(0.000,0.000)	(0.000,0.000)	(0.000,0.000)	(0.000,0.000)
04Q1	(0.000,0.000)	(0.000,0.000)	(0.000,0.000)	(0.000,0.000)	(0.000,0.000)
04Q2	(0.000,0.000)	(0.000,0.000)	(0.000,0.000)	(0.000,0.000)	(0.000,0.000)
04Q3	(0.000,0.000)	(0.000,0.000)	(0.000,0.000)	(0.000,0.000)	(0.000,0.000)
04Q4	(0.000,0.000)	(0.000,0.000)	(0.000,0.000)	(0.000,0.000)	(0.000,0.000)
05Q1	(0.000,0.000)	(0.000,0.000)	(0.000,0.000)	(0.000,0.000)	(0.000,0.000)
05Q2	(0.000,0.000)	(0.000,0.000)	(0.000,0.000)	(0.000,0.000)	(0.000,0.000)
05Q3	(0.000,0.000)	(0.000,0.000)	(0.000,0.000)	(0.000,0.000)	(0.000,0.000)
05Q4	(0.000,0.000)	(0.000,0.000)	(0.000,0.000)	(0.000,0.000)	(0.000,0.000)
06Q1	(0.000,0.000)	(0.000,0.000)	(0.000,0.000)	(0.000,0.000)	(0.000,0.000)
06Q2	(0.000,0.000)	(0.000,0.000)	(0.000,0.000)	(0.000,0.000)	(0.000,0.000)
06Q3	(0.000,0.000)	(0.000,0.000)	(0.000,0.000)	(0.000,0.000)	(0.000,0.000)
06Q4	(0.000,0.000)	(0.000,0.000)	(0.000,0.000)	(0.000,0.000)	(0.000,0.000)
07Q1	(0.000,0.000)	(0.000,0.000)	(0.000,0.000)	(0.000,0.000)	(0.000,0.000)
07Q2	(0.000,0.000)	(0.000,0.000)	(0.000,0.000)	(0.000,0.000)	(0.000,0.000)
07Q3	(0.000,0.000)	(0.000,0.000)	(0.000,0.000)	(0.000,0.000)	(0.000,0.000)
07Q4	(0.000,0.000)	(0.000,0.000)	(0.000,0.000)	(0.000,0.000)	(0.000,0.000)
08Q1	(0.000,0.000)	(0.000,0.000)	(0.000,0.000)	(0.000,0.000)	(0.000,0.000)
08Q2	(0.000,0.000)	(0.000,0.000)	(0.000,0.000)	(0.000,0.000)	(0.000,0.000)
08Q3	(0.000,0.004)	(0.000,0.004)	(0.000,0.004)	(0.000,0.004)	(0.000,0.004)
08Q4	(0.006,0.004)	(0.006,0.004)	(0.006,0.004)	(0.003,0.002)	(0.003,0.002)
09Q1	(0.000,0.004)	(0.000,0.004)	(0.000,0.004)	(0.000,0.003)	(0.000,0.003)
09Q2	(0.006,0.004)	(0.006,0.004)	(0.006,0.004)	(0.005,0.003)	(0.004,0.003)
09Q3	(0.006,0.013)	(0.006,0.013)	(0.006,0.013)	(0.006,0.013)	(0.006,0.013)

(Continued)

Table 3.9 (Continued)

	Observed bank failure	Predicted bank failure rates			
Quarter	rates	Model A	Model B	Model C	Model D
09Q4	(0.013,0.009)	(0.013,0.009)	(0.013,0.009)	(0.014,0.010)	(0.014,0.011)
10Q1	(0.007,0.009)	(0.007,0.009)	(0.007,0.009)	(0.007,0.011)	(0.007,0.010)
10Q2	(0.000,0.009)	(0.000,0.009)	(0.000,0.009)	(0.000,0.010)	(0.000,0.010)
10Q3	(0.000,0.000)	(0.000,0.000)	(0.000,0.000)	(0.003,0.004)	(0.002,0.003)
10Q4	(0.000,0.000)	(0.000,0.000)	(0.000,0.000)	(0.002,0.003)	(0.003,0.004)
11Q1	(0.000,0.000)	(0.000,0.000)	(0.000,0.000)	(0.000,0.000)	(0.000,0.000)
11Q2	(0.000,0.005)	(0.000,0.005)	(0.000,0.005)	(0.000,0.007)	(0.000,0.006)
11Q3	(0.000,0.000)	(0.000,0.000)	(0.000,0.000)	(0.000,0.000)	(0.000,0.000)
11Q4	(0.000,0.000)	(0.000,0.000)	(0.000,0.000)	(0.000,0.000)	(0.000,0.000)
12Q1	(0.000,0.000)	(0.000,0.000)	(0.000,0.000)	(0.000,0.000)	(0.000,0.000)
12Q2	(0.000,0.005)	(0.000,0.005)	(0.000,0.005)	(0.000,0.007)	(0.000,0.006)
12Q3	(0.000,0.005)	(0.000,0.005)	(0.000,0.005)	(0.000,0.005)	(0.000,0.006)
12Q4	(0.000,0.000)	(0.000,0.000)	(0.000,0.000)	(0.000,0.000)	(0.000,0.000)

Model A to D bank failures (2002–2012)

Table 3.9 also displays the marginal contribution of the LIBOR-OISS in predicting bank failures. Columns 2, 3, and 5 show the observed one-year conditional bank failure rates against the predicted values from model A and model C, which excludes the LIBOR-OISS. The differences between the predictions of these two models are substantial for 2009 and 2010. In particular, as can be seen from the aforementioned columns, there are significant differences between the predicted failure rates of models A and C in 2009 and 2010.[96,97]

Columns 2, 3, and 6 in Table 3.9 display the observed one-year conditional bank failure rates against the predicted values from model A and model D, which excludes liquidity risk. The differences between the predictions of these two models are substantial for 2009 and 2010. Because model C excludes the LIBOR-OISS, the differences between the predicted values of models A and C measure the marginal contribution of the LIBOR-OISS. Furthermore, as can be seen from Table 3.9, the predicted values of models C and D are very close to each other, suggesting that the LIBOR-OISS accounts for a majority of the marginal contribution of liquidity risk.[98,99]

3.4 Policy Implications for Basel III Liquidity Regulation and Bank Failure

In this section, we consider the impact of monetary policy transmission and compliance with the LCR and NSFR standards from Basel III liquidity regulation.

3.4.1 The Impact on Monetary Policy Transmission for Class I and II Banks

Class II sample banks that have relatively large maturity mismatches as measured by the NSFR shortfall in Section 3.2.3, are most affected by contractionary monetary policy shocks For instance, in general, a reduction of total loans by 0.17% follows an increase of 1% in the short-term interest rate.

Class I banks with smaller NSFR shortfalls are able to increase their lending by 0.18%, following an increase in the interest rate. This follows from the fact that the 391 banks are mostly intra-group liquidity providers. Also, we find that the degree of asset liquidity is not relevant for bank lending channel identification. However, Class II banks that are funded through relatively unstable sources by the LCR are better prepared to mitigate monetary policy risk than other Class II banks.

3.4.2 Compliance with the Basel III Standards

The LCR and NSFR can be useful prudential tools and relatively easy to implement for jurisdictions that do not want to rely solely on risk sensitive capital requirements. Combining the LCR and NSFR with Basel-type capital rules can reduce the risk of depleted liquidity in banks. As the findings in this chapter showed, however, policy makers need to be cognizant of the inherent limitations and weaknesses of the LCR and NSFR. Also, the LCR standard requires more HQLAs to be held that, *ceteris parabis*, may lower returns. This may incentivize excessive risk-taking in certain spheres of the economy. These are some reasons for concluding that whilst the BCBS has gone a long way in addressing liquidity risks, its efforts still remain a modest milestone in combating liquidity risks in prudential supervision. Furthermore, in some jurisdictions, sovereign bonds are highly risky and even potentially subject to default risk not captured consistently by rating agencies. All-encompassing regulations could, in severe cases, see liquidity regulation actually contributing to bank insolvency.

Furthermore, we consider the potential effects that complying with the Basel III liquidity standards may have on monetary policy transmission. Firstly, satisfying NSFR requirements would reduce the importance of the bank lending channel among both Class I and II banks. This is due to the fact that they would be better prepared to counteract the tightening of monetary policy. However, complying with the LCR would only reduce the relevance of this channel for banks with a small NSFR shortfall whilst it would increase for the others (see, Subsection 3.2.3 for further detail). Here, we argue that a higher LCR shortfall is related to a larger funding base relative to the HQLA stock. Thus, smaller LCR shortfalls would tend to reduce the funds available for stimulating loan growth.

If Class I and II banks already have deficient stable funding, the reaction of loan supply to monetary policy tightening should be enhanced. Bank level data provides limited information on the manner in which LCR and NSFR would change monetary policy transmission. The information becomes less reliable with an increase in the impact of Basel III regulation on banks' balance sheets.

3.5 Implications of Basel III Liquidity Regulation and Bank Failure

In this section, we draw the most important conclusions about the results obtained in preceding sections, where global banking data for 391 LIBOR-based banks in 38 countries for the period 2002 through 2012 was discussed.[100]

3.5.1 Implications (Approximations of Basel III and Traditional Liquidity Risk Measures)

Most importantly, we approximate the Basel III standards, LCR and NSFR, which are measures of asset liquidity and funding stability, respectively, for global EMERG banking data mentioned earlier (see Question 3.1.1 of

Subsection 3.1.3). This is a challenging task given the nature of the data available and the ever-changing nature of Basel III liquidity regulation.

In the light of the determined results, our analysis gives us a new understanding of the problem of approximating liquidity risk measures. From Figures 3.1 and 3.2, we observe that the NSFR for Class I banks increased during the 2007 through 2009 financial crisis. This appears to be counter-intuitive as we are aware that liquidity decreased drastically during this time. This brings the effectiveness of NSFR as a Basel III measure of liquidity risk into question. Class I and II banks behave very similarly up to the onset of the financial crisis. This may be due to the lack of differentiation of banks in terms of liquidity. From 09Q2 to 12Q4 there was a steady increase in the LCR. This is probably due to banks holding more liquid assets and restricting cash outflows and risky activities.

In this paragraph, we highlight how our research on approximating Basel III and traditional liquidity risk measures has advanced the knowledge in this field of endeavor. For both Class I and II banks, our research approximates liquidity measures for a large diversity of banks for an extended period (i.e., 02Q1 to 12Q4) on a global scale. The negative correlation between the NSFR for Class I banks and the actual market and idiosyncratic liquidity during the crisis was an unexpected contribution to existing knowledge. The relationship between banking distress and Class I and II bank LCR as well as Class II NSFR was as expected and adds credence to the Basel III rationale. The disparity between the dynamics of liquidity risk measures for Class I and II banks subsequent to the 2007 to 2009 financial crisis may be attributed to injections of liquidity via bailout plans that seemed to have favored Class I ("too-big-to-fail" banks) above Class II banks.

In the sequel, we analyze some of our results in the light of existing literature on approximating Basel III and traditional liquidity risk measures. No prior studies have attempted to achieve the aforementioned approximations using global public data (see Subsection 3.2.1). Several studies have approximated these liquidity risk measures for U.S. public data.[101,102] Also, the current chapter incorporates the prescripts of BCBS238 (January 2013) for approximating the LCR.[103] We believe that this makes our computations more consistent with regulation and closer to reality. Notwithstanding this, the aforementioned literature points to the fact that the LCR is biased toward government bonds. This may negate lending to the private sector in an environment where budget deficits are sizeable. However, this bias may be useful in terms of interest rate risk when encouraging prospective investors. The dynamics of the NPAR in Figure 3.2 suggests that it is a strong indicator of banking distress. This is verified by the fact that the NPAR rose sharply during the 2007 to 2009 financial crisis. In the same period, the average ROA decreased dramatically, which is what is expected during stress scenarios. Improving profitability subsequent to the crisis has accompanied economic recovery in most countries. From Figure 3.2, it is clear that the LIBOR-OISS is a good predictor of bank distress (compare with subsequent discussions on LIBOR-OISS). On the other hand, besides its reasonable ability to predict bank failure (see Table 3.5), there does not seem to be an easily verifiable relationship between the BIITKR and the bank distress experienced during the financial crisis. In some sense, this adds credibility to the view that capital adequacy was sufficient before, during, and after the crisis.

Future research on Basel III and traditional liquidity risk measure approximation will entail fine tuning the methodology employed in this chapter. The process may be aided by the availability of more suitable data of sufficient granularity as well as improved extrapolation and interpolation techniques.

3.5.2 Implications (Key Statistics of Basel III and Traditional Liquidity Risk Measures)

We are able to make conclusions about the descriptive statistics of Basel III and traditional liquidity risk measures (see Question 3.1.2 in Subsection 3.1.3). For instance, in Table 3.1 for Class I banks, three out of four variables show positive skewness (LCR, NSFR, and BDR), while GSR is negatively skewed. The value of the kurtosis for all the variables in Table 3.1 is equal to or less than 3, which means that the distribution is flat. All risk measures show forms of normality because the probability values in the said table have p-values greater than 5%. Nevertheless, the test for normality is sensitive to the number of observations. This may be problematic when it comes to determining key statistics. This is also true for Class II banks.

From Table 3.1, it is clear that most banks seem to have satisfied the Basel III minimum liquidity standard of 100% with respect to the NSFR for the latter part of the 2002 through 2012 period. On the other hand, it is hard to conclude that Basel III LCR standards were complied with most of the time.

Future research on Basel III and traditional liquidity risk measure key statistics will involve describing the statistics of improved risk measure data. A more meaningful comparison between the descriptive statistics of Class I and Class II banks may be possible. A wider range of tests may also be done and existing econometric models may be applied. Here, the heterogeneity of the 391 sample banks complicates matters.

3.5.3 Implications (LCR and NSFR Shortfalls)

In Subsection 3.2.4, we determine the shortfalls of the Basel III liquidity standards, LCR and NSFR, for Class I and II banks. Here, Question 3.1.3 is answered, where Basel III standards were set at 100% (see Figure 3.3 for more information).

We argue that a higher LCR shortfall can be associated with an enhanced funding base relative to HQLAs. In essence, decreased LCR shortfalls would tend to reduce the funds available for stimulating loan growth.

From our results, we observe that LCR and NSFR shortfalls are not necessarily additive. In this regard, we note that depending on the steps, decreasing the shortfall in one standard may result in a similar decrease in the shortfall of the other.[104,105] As expected, with the introduction of Basel III liquidity standards, LCR and NSFR shortfalls decreased drastically in recent times. The connections between the aforementioned shortfalls and monetary policy are explained in LCR and NSFR Shortfalls, p. 60.

A next step in our research on LCR and NSFR shortfalls will involve determining the implications of the following actions. To satisfy the Basel III LCR standard, banks will in all likelihood increase holdings of low-yielding assets. To meet the NSFR of Basel III, banks may have to increase the average maturity of its liabilities. In both cases, the new liquidity requirements are assumed to exercise downward pressure on profitability and, thus, upward pressure on lending margins.[106] As a result, there will be a negative impact on LCR and NSFR shortfalls, and they may increase.

3.5.4 Implications (Comparison with BCBS and EBA Results)

Although difficult at times, we are able to compare parts of our investigation to previous quantitative impact studies (see Question 3.1.4 in Subsection 3.1.3). Since our study is based on time-series EMERG global liquidity data[107] that is richer than single date data, we cannot directly compare our results with those of the BCBS[108–112] and the EBA.[113–116] However, our results are broadly consistent with the results of these studies that were based on private cross sectional data because the banks participating in the BCBS and EBA studies tend to have similar defining features.[117] On the other hand, there is more variation in our sample, that includes 391 banks of various sizes and capital holdings over a 11-year period. The larger sample size and the longer sample period allow us to perform additional analyses that were not possible in the BCBS and EBA studies (see Question 3.1.4 for further perspectives).

In our study, we are able to determine the sensitivity of the Basel III and traditional liquidity risk measures to some degree. As was mentioned before, there are gaps between the EMERG global liquidity data and data required for calculating the LCR and NSFR especially in respect of granularity and certain OBS items. As a consequence, it is likely that our results are less accurate than those for the BCBS and EBA quantitative studies.

Future comparative research will involve considering updated data from the BCBS and EBA in the spirit of previous quantitative impact studies. We believe that these future studies will enhance our understanding of the impact of Basel III liquidity regulation on sovereign economies.

3.5.5 Implications (Information Values for Liquidity Risk Measures)

In Subsection 3.3.1, we find that the Basel III liquidity risk measures, LCR and NSFR, have relatively low information values when compared with traditional liquidity risk measures such as the NPAR, ROA, LIBOR-OISS, BIITKR, GSR, and BDR (refer to Question 3.1.5 in Subsection 3.1.3).[118]

In this chapter, the information value is a measure of a variable's ability to discriminate between two performance outcomes in prediction modeling. This approach follows the literature rather closely.[119] If we trace this line of thought back even further, we find that our information value is a variant of Kullback–Leibler divergence statistics (also known as information divergence or relative entropy), which is a measure of the difference between two probability distributions, in information theory and statistics.[120]

Future research on Basel III and traditional liquidity risk measure information values will entail sharpening the valuation techniques in order to obtain more accurate results. This process will involve employing more advanced probabilistic methodologies.

3.5.6 Implications (Bank Failure Rates)

Our empirical results show that, in general, failure rates were highest during and after the 2007 to 2009 financial crisis (Question 3.1.6 in Subsection 3.1.3).

Our empirical results show that the probability of failure is negatively correlated with the LCR for both Class I and II banks. On the other hand, Class I bank failure probability is positively and Class II banks negatively correlated with the NSFR. If the result providing information about the connection between Class I bank failure and the NSFR is not caused by the inaccuracy of the approximation technique, it would imply that this measure is a poor indicator of bank distress (see Question 3.1.6 in Subsection 3.1.3). Furthermore, we argue that the LCR requirement may support the goals of effective liquidity regulation and negate issues of systemic risk.

3.5.7 Implications (Estimating Discrete-Time Hazard Models)

We estimate a discrete time hazard model[121] for Class I and II banks that differentiates between idiosyncratic and market-wide liquidity risks (see Question 3.1.7 in Subsection 3.1.3).

Our approach is consistent with the literature where liquidity risk is divided into idiosyncratic liquidity risk and aggregate liquidity risk.[122]

However, a future advance could be to improve the discrete-time hazard model considered in this chapter in order to discuss further features of bank failure. Also, the model may investigate other variables that may be more appropriate for studying bank failure.[123]

3.5.8 Implications (Contribution of Liquidity Risk to Bank Failure)

Our empirical results show that, in models A and C, the probability of failure is negatively correlated with the LCR for both Class I and II banks, whereas Class I bank failure probability is positively and Class II banks are negatively correlated with the NSFR. Because the LCR is a measure of asset liquidity, whereas the NSFR is a measure of funding stability, these results highlight the subtle difference between the two. Here, high funding stability for Class II banks reduces the probability of bank failure, whereas liquidity hoarding has the negative externality that increases the probability of bank failure.[124,125] From the aforementioned, the overall impression is that, at this stage, the NSFR is a weak measure because it depends upon the ability of banks to model investor behavior that may be stable or unstable during a crisis. This criticism should be addressed by the BCBS in future. Also, we estimate a bank failure model that differentiates between idiosyncratic and systemic funding liquidity risks. We find that the latter was the major predictor of bank failures in 2009 and 2010, whereas idiosyncratic liquidity risk played only a minor role. This finding implies that an effective liquidity risk management framework needs to target banks at both the individual and the systemic level.[126]

For Class I and II banks, the results of Table 3.8 suggest that market-wide liquidity risk as encapsulated by LIBOR-OISS was a major predictor of bank failures in 2009 and 2010. On the other hand, the approximate LCR and NSFR measures had very little ability to predict bank failures for Class I and II banks. In other words, idiosyncratic liquidity risk played only a minimal role. The predicted failure rate of model C is lower than that of model A in 2009, whereas it is higher than that of model A in 2010. We offer the following explanation. By looking at Table 3.8 again, we see that the LIBOR-OISS was extremely high in 2008 and was extremely low in 2009. The former caused more banks to fail in 2009. The extremely low LIBOR-OISS (perhaps because of Central Bank interventions) in 2009 helped reduce the number of bank failures in 2010. This explanation provides an answer to Question 3.1.8 in Subsection 3.1.3.[127]

3.5.9 Implications (Policy Implications for Basel III Liquidity Regulation and Bank Failure)

In Subsection 3.4.2, we allude to policy implications that involve the LCR and NSFR for Class I and II banks (see Question 3.1.9 in Subsection 3.1.3).

The aforementioned policy implications mainly involve monetary policy transmission and differ very significantly from jurisdiction to jurisdiction. As the recent financial crises showed, the BCBS needs to recognize the inherent limitations and weaknesses of liquidity provisioning. The proposals at an international level to supplement Basel III liquidity risk measures with other internationally harmonized and appropriately calibrated liquidity standards have been welcomed. This could lead to Basel III adoption by a wide range of countries in the future. The LCR and NSFR cannot do the job alone; it needs to be complemented by other prudential tools or measures to ensure a comprehensive attack on liquidity dissipation in both the banking and broader financial sectors. Additional measures to provide a comprehensive view of aggregate liquidity, including embedded liquidity, and to trigger enhanced surveillance by supervisors need to be developed. There appears to be consensus that no single tool or measure would have prevented the financial crisis and that an adequate policy response requires a variety of macroprudential and microprudential policy tools.

Future Basel III-related policy should integrate the various components contributing to bank failure in order to develop a better strategy for combating this phenomenon in Class I and II banks. Of particular interest would be the integration of procyclicality, risk management, leverage, and capital into the Basel III liquidity framework. Each of these supplementary policies should help to prevent future bank distress. The too-big-to-fail principle that saved systemically important Class I banks from failure should also be revisited.

3.6 How to Obtain the Results in Chapter 3

In this section, we provide hints on how to obtain the results in Chapter 3.

3.6.1 How to Obtain Information Values for Liquidity Risk Measures

Our approach to information values follows the contribution in Thomas et al.[128] In their methodology, they divide the value of each liquidity risk measure into 10 deciles and calculate its information value as follows:

$$IV = \sum_{i=1}^{10}(P_{bad}^i - P_{good}^i)log\frac{P_{bad}^i}{P_{good}^i}$$

In this equation, $P_{bad}^i = \dfrac{N_b^i}{N_b}$ is the proportion of the number of "bad" banks in interval i, N_b^i to the total number of bad banks in the entire sample, N_b. Analogously, $P_{good}^i = \dfrac{N_g^i}{N_g}$ is the proportion of "good" banks in interval i, N_g^i to the total number of good banks in the entire sample, N_g.

3.6.2 How to Obtain the Insolvency and Liquidity Risk Components

The following insolvency and liquidity risk models were introduced by Wu and Hong (Wu and Hong 2012b). In banking, the concepts of liquidity and solvency are intertwined and often indistinguishable. An insolvent bank can easily become illiquid, whereas an illiquid one can become insolvent.[129] In this subsection, we discuss issues related to the relationship between liquidity, insolvency, and bank failures. In particular, we estimate a discrete-time hazard model, in which the conditional bank failure rate is linked to insolvency and liquidity risks.[130] In this model, the log-hazard, h_{t+1}^i is specified as

$$h_{t+1}^i = \alpha^0 + R_{t+1}^{li} + R_{t+1}^{Li}, \qquad (3.1)$$

where α^0, R_{t+1}^{Ii}, and R_{t+1}^{Li} is a constant, an insolvency risk term and a liquidity risk term, respectively.

3.6.2.1 Insolvency Risk Term

It is well-known that variables affecting bank insolvency risk include capital adequacy, asset quality, profitability, and local economic conditions.[131] In this case, we specify the insolvency term as

$$R_{t+1}^{Ii} = \alpha^1 \frac{A_t^{bi}}{E_t^{ci} + R_t^i} \frac{\pi_t^i}{r_t^{di}} + \alpha^2 \frac{K_t^{bi} - E_t^{ci}}{E_t^{ci} + R_t^i} + \alpha^3 \frac{\Lambda_t^i - r_t^{\Lambda i}}{E_t^{ci} + R_t^i} + \alpha^4 \frac{S_t^i - r_t^{Si}}{E_t^{ci} + R_t^i}$$

$$+ \alpha^5 \frac{X_t^{lbi}}{E_t^{ci} + R_t^i} + \alpha^6 \frac{I_t^{nnbi}}{E_t^{ci} + R_t^i} + \alpha^7 \frac{A_t^{ni}}{E_t^{ci} + R_t^i}$$

$$+ \alpha^8 \frac{A_t^{ni}}{E_t^{ci} + R_t^i} \Delta H_t^i + \alpha^9 \frac{A_t^{ni}}{E_t^{ci} + R_t^i} \Delta U_t^i \qquad (3.2)$$

The first component in (3.2) is the market valuation component, $\frac{A_t^{bi}}{E_t^{ci} + R_t^i} \frac{\pi_t^i}{r_t^{di}}$, where $\frac{A_t^{bi}}{E_t^{ci} + R_t^i}$ is the ratio of a bank's total asset book value, A_t^{bi}, to the sum of its tangible common equity, E_t^{ci}, and loan and lease loss reserves, R_t^i. Since the aforementioned sum can be regarded as the effective capital of a bank, $\frac{A_t^{bi}}{E_t^{ci} + R_t^i}$ is a measure of leverage. Also, $\frac{\pi_t^i}{r_t^{di}}$ is the ratio of ROA, π_t^i, to the market discount rate, r_t^{di}. The leverage term $\frac{A_t^{bi}}{E_t^{ci} + R_t^i}$, serves as an amplifier for the effects of changes in π_t^i and r_t^{di}.[132]

The second component, $\frac{K_t^{bi} - E_t^{ci}}{E_t^{ci} + R_t^i}$, is the ratio of intangible capital, $K_t^{bi} - E_t^{ci}$, to effective capital, $E_t^{ci} + R_t^i$, with the book value of capital, K_t^{bi}, and tangible common equity, E_t^{ci}.

The third component, $\frac{\Lambda_t^i - r_t^{\Lambda i}}{E_t^{ci} + R_t^i}$, is the ratio of the interest income from loans, $\Lambda_t^i - r_t^{\Lambda i}$, to effective capital, $E_t^{ci} + R_t^i$, where loan yields and total loans are denoted by $r_t^{\Lambda i}$ and Λ_t^i, respectively.[133]

Similarly, the fourth component, $\dfrac{S_t^i - r_t^{Si}}{E_t^{ci} + R_t^i}$, is the ratio of interest income from securities, $r_t^{Si} S_t^i$ to effective capital, $E_t^{ci} + R_t^i$.

The fifth component, $\dfrac{X_t^{Ibi}}{E_t^{ci} + R_t^i}$, is the ratio of interest expense, X_t^{Ibi}, to effective capital, $E_t^{ci} + R_t^i$.

The sixth component, $\dfrac{I_t^{nnbi}}{E_t^{ci} + R_t^i}$, is the ratio of net noninterest income, I_t^{nnbi}, to effective capital, $E_t^{ci} + R_t^i$.

The seventh component is the NPAR, $\dfrac{A_t^{ni}}{E_t^{ci} + R_t^i}$, that is, the ratio of nonperforming assets, A_t^{ni}, to effective capital, $E_t^{ci} + R_t^i$.

The eighth component, $\dfrac{A_t^{ni}}{E_t^{ci} + R_t^i} \Delta H_t^i$, is the interaction term between the NPAR, $\dfrac{A_t^{ni}}{E_t^{ci} + R_t^i}$, and the change in housing price indices, ΔH_t^i.[134]

We expect α^9 associated with $\dfrac{A_t^{ni}}{E_t^{ci} + R_t^i} \Delta U_t^i$, the interaction term between the NPAR and the change in unemployment rates, ΔU_t^i, to be positive because a high unemployment rate would increase the severity of the loss.[135]

3.6.2.2 Liquidity Risk Term

The liquidity risk term consists of two parts.[136] The first is the idiosyncratic component that provides information about the strength of liquidity risk management in banks. For instance, a bank with stronger liquidity risk management is less exposed to idiosyncratic risk. The second component is the market-wide liquidity risk that comes from the market and affects every bank.[137] For example, for many banks, a severe market liquidity disruption could cause a shortage of funding. In this case, the component attributed to liquidity risk is specified as

$$R_{t+1}^{Li} = \alpha^{10} O_t^i + \alpha^{11} C_t^{Ri} + \alpha^{12} F_t^{Ri} \qquad (3.3)$$

The LIBOR-OISS, O_t^s, measures the market-wide liquidity risk. We expect the coefficient on the LIBOR-OISS, a^{10}, to be positive, as a rise in the LIBOR-OISS would increase the market funding liquidity risk. The LCR and NSFR measure the idiosyncratic liquidity risk. We expect the coefficient of the LCR, a^{11}, to be negative as banks with more liquid assets are less likely to encounter liquidity difficulties.[138] For both Class I and II banks, our results do, in fact, yield a negative coefficient for the LCR. Finally, the coefficient of the NSFR, a^{11}, is also expected to be negative as banks with more stable funding are less likely to run into funding problems. Here, our results yield a negative coefficient for Class II banks, whereas the coefficient is positive for Class banks. This is an anomaly that may inform future regulatory reform regarding the calculation of the components of the NSFR. In all likelihood, the too-big-to-fail phenomenon has a role to play here.

3.6.3 How to Obtain the Discrete-Time Hazard Model

From the previous subsection, we have that the discrete-time hazard model used to investigate bank failure—hereafter known as Model A—can be determined as follows.[139] Substituting (3.2) and (3.3) into equation (3.1), we obtain

$$
\begin{aligned}
h_{t+1}^i = {} & \alpha^0 + \alpha^1 \frac{A_t^{bi}}{E_t^{ci} + R_t^i} \frac{\pi_t^i}{r_t^{di}} + \alpha^2 \frac{K_t^{bi} - E_t^{ci}}{E_t^{ci} + R_t^i} + \alpha^3 \frac{\Lambda_t^i r_t^{\Lambda i}}{E_t^{ci} + R_t^i} + \alpha^4 \frac{S_t^i r_t^{Si}}{E_t^{ci} + R_t^i} \\
& + \alpha^5 \frac{X_t^{lbi}}{E_t^{ci} + R_t^i} + \alpha^6 \frac{I_t^{nnbi}}{E_t^{ci} + R_t^i} + \alpha^7 \frac{A_t^{ni}}{E_t^{ci} + R_t^i} + \alpha^8 \frac{A_t^{ni}}{E_t^{ci} + R_t^i} \Delta H_t^i \\
& + \alpha^9 \frac{A_t^{ni}}{E_t^{ci} + R_t^i} \Delta U_t^i + \alpha^{10} O_t^s + \alpha^{11} C_t^{Ri} + \alpha^{12} F_t^{Ri}.
\end{aligned}
$$

The first to ninth components in (3.2) correspond to those stipulated in the previous equation. From this model, we can derive Model B, Model C and Model D, where LCR and NSFR, LIBOR-OISS and liquidity risk are excluded, respectively.[140] In essence, this means that Models B through D can be represented by the equations

$$h_{t+1}^{Bi} = \alpha^0 + \alpha^{1'} \frac{A_t^{bi}}{E_t^{ci} + R_t^i} \frac{\pi_t^i}{r_t^{di}} + \alpha^2 \frac{K_t^{bi} - E_t^{ci}}{E_t^{ci} + R_t^i} + \alpha^3 \frac{\Lambda_t^i - r_t^{\Lambda i}}{E_t^{ci} + R_t^i} + \alpha^4 \frac{S_t^i - r_t^{Si}}{E_t^{ci} + R_t^i}$$

$$+ \alpha^5 \frac{X_t^{lbi}}{E_t^{ci} + R_t^i} + \alpha^6 \frac{I_t^{nnbi}}{E_t^{ci} + R_t^i} + \alpha^7 \frac{A_t^{ni}}{E_t^{ci} + R_t^i} + \alpha^8 \frac{A_t^{ni}}{E_t^{ci} + R_t^i} \Delta H_t^i$$

$$+ \alpha^9 \frac{A_t^{ni}}{E_t^{ci} + R_t^i} \Delta U_t^i + \alpha^{10} O_t^8$$

$$h_{t+1}^{Ci} = \alpha^0 + \alpha^{1'} \frac{A_t^{bi}}{E_t^{ci} + R_t^i} \frac{\pi_t^i}{r_t^{di}} + \alpha^2 \frac{K_t^{bi} - E_t^{ci}}{E_t^{ci} + R_t^i} + \alpha^3 \frac{\Lambda_t^i - r_t^{\Lambda i}}{E_t^{ci} + R_t^i} + \alpha^4 \frac{S_t^i - r_t^{Si}}{E_t^{ci} + R_t^i}$$

$$+ \alpha^5 \frac{X_t^{lbi}}{E_t^{ci} + R_t^i} + \alpha^6 \frac{I_t^{nnbi}}{E_t^{ci} + R_t^i} + \alpha^7 \frac{A_t^{ni}}{E_t^{ci} + R_t^i} + \alpha^8 \frac{A_t^{ni}}{E_t^{ci} + R_t^i} \Delta H_t^i$$

$$+ \alpha^9 \frac{A_t^{ni}}{E_t^{ci} + R_t^i} \Delta U_t^i + \alpha^{11} C_t^{Ri} + \alpha^{12} F_t^{Ri}$$

and

$$h_{t+1}^{Di} = \alpha^0 + \alpha^{1'} \frac{A_t^{bi}}{E_t^{ci} + R_t^i} \frac{\pi_t^i}{r_t^{di}} + \alpha^2 \frac{K_t^{bi} - E_t^{ci}}{E_t^{ci} + R_t^i} + \alpha^3 \frac{\Lambda_t^i - r_t^{\Lambda i}}{E_t^{ci} + R_t^i} + \alpha^4 \frac{S_t^i - r_t^{Si}}{E_t^{ci} + R_t^i}$$

$$+ \alpha^5 \frac{X_t^{lbi}}{E_t^{ci} + R_t^i} + \alpha^6 \frac{I_t^{nnbi}}{E_t^{ci} + R_t^i} + \alpha^7 \frac{A_t^{ni}}{E_t^{ci} + R_t^i} + \alpha^8 \frac{A_t^{ni}}{E_t^{ci} + R_t^i} \Delta H_t^i$$

$$+ \alpha^9 \frac{A_t^{ni}}{E_t^{ci} + R_t^i} \Delta U_t^i$$

respectively.[141]

CHAPTER 4

Basel III Liquidity Creation and Bank Capital

Liquidity creation refers to a banks' function of extending illiquid loans to borrowers while providing depositors with the opportunity to withdraw funds upon demand at par value.[1-4] In this chapter, we first determine how to analyze the connections between liquidity creation and bank capital. By using a Granger causality approach, we investigate the causal relationship between *bank capital* and *liquidity creation*[5] (broad and narrow measure) and its directionality in large, medium, and small banks.[6] Second, we are interested in the risks that liquidity creation generates for the bank. In a Basel III context, various aspects of such risk are taken into account by incorporating earnings volatility, credit risk, and nonperforming loans. Additionally, size, market share, inflation, and unemployment were included as controls.

4.1 Background to Basel III, Liquidity Creation and Bank Capital

A Granger causality model is used to characterize the causal relation between banks' capital and liquidity creation. Also, the Granger causality results will identify those variables that are systemically important. In this case, regulators will be able to specifically target the variables that are important for improved liquidity regulation.

4.1.1 Review of Basel III, Liquidity Creation and Bank Capital

In lieu of impending Basel III liquidity regulation, we consider empirical studies that investigate pivotal concepts such as liquidity, bank capital regulation, risk, Granger causality, and bank size. Furthermore, a succinct overview of the theories that form the basis for our research is discussed.

We apply the liquidity creation *formula* of Berger and Bouwman[7] to a 2002 to 2012 sample of global banks. By contrast, Berger et al.[8] investigates the effects of regulatory interventions and capital support on bank risk taking and liquidity creation by using a unique dataset of German universal banks from 1999 to 2009. They show that regulation and capital support result in statistically significant reductions in risk taking and liquidity creation in the short and long run. Furthermore, in a recent overview, Berger and coauthors[9] agree with earlier postulations[10,11] that liquidity creation is, in fact, a core function of banks and becomes even more crucial to the economy during financial crises.

In essence, the creation of liquidity exposes banks to an array of risks. Many studies consider the relation between liquidity creation and various forms of risk using banking data from different countries. In this regard, we are cognizant of the impact of risk and, as such, include the control variables *credit risk, earnings volatility, z-score,* and *nonperforming loans* in our study.

Horvath, Seidler, and Weill conduct a Granger causality test in a dynamic GMM panel estimator framework on an exhaustive data set of mainly small Czech banks from 2000 to 2010.[12] Their study analyzes the potential impact on liquidity creation of tighter capital requirements such as those in Basel III. They postulate that there is a trade-off between the benefits of financial stability induced by stronger capital requirements and the benefits of greater liquidity creation. In other words, any action favoring one objective would negatively impact the other. This would suggest that potentially Basel III can reduce bank liquidity creation by introducing tighter capital requirements. Horvath et al., further support the view that greater liquidity creation may hamper bank solvency.[13] Our choice of control variables, *viz.*, capital, credit risk, z-score, earnings volatility, nonperforming loans, size, market share, inflation, and unemployment, for liquidity creation and capital correspond to that of Horthvath et al.[14]

Specifically, like Horvath et al.[15] and Berger and Bouman,[16] *we also* consider how bank capital and liquidity creation (broad and narrow measure) affect all the aforementioned control variables and vice versa in large, medium, and small banks using the Granger causality model in lieu of Basel III. Our study differs in terms of the type of data, duration as well as type and number of banks considered. In particular, we use time series quarterly data for the period 2002 to 2012 obtained from 391 London Interbank Offered Rate (LIBOR)-based large, medium, and small banks from 38 countries.

Furthermore, the relationship between bank capital and liquidity measured for on-balance sheet (BS) activities is investigated by Distinguin et al.[17] They utilize a simultaneous equations framework using 2000 to 2006 European and U.S. publicly traded commercial bank data. The authors show that banks decrease their regulatory capital ratios when they face higher illiquidity as defined in Basel III or when they create more liquidity. Also, they emphasized the importance of regulating large banks that behave differently from smaller ones. By contrast to the simultaneous equations framework, the current chapter investigates how bank capital affects liquidity creation and vice versa by using Granger causality techniques. Like Distinguin et al.[18] we also consider the impact of bank size.

Moreover, we focus on empirical studies considering the relationship between capital and liquidity creation together with the impact of bank size. Berger and Bouman[19] make a major contribution to this topic by suggesting a new method for measuring the liquidity created by banks for a sample of U.S. commercial banks from 1993 to 2003. They propose a classification of all BS items as liquid, semiliquid, or illiquid (see Table 2.1 for more information). This classification applies to banks' assets, liabilities, equity, and off-balance-sheet (OBS) activities.

For large banks, as capital increases or decreases, liquidity creation will increase or decrease. By contrast, for small banks, as capital decreases or increases, liquidity creation will increase or decrease. Berger and Bouwman[20] also emphasize the differences brought about by changes in the type of liquidity creation. This pioneering article has triggered some recent studies on the same topic.[21–23] In our contribution, we generally follow the methodology suggested by Berger and Bouwman[24] but extend their analysis to include liquidity creation and bank capital data for large, medium, and small banks on a global scale rather than just for the United States. Our analysis includes, amongst other things, visual inspection, descriptive statistics, stationarity tests, and the Granger causality analysis.

The theoretical perspectives underpinning our current study hinge upon two main opposing hypotheses. In this regard, the papers by

Diamond and Rajan[25,26] and others suggest that banks with higher capital ratios may create less liquidity because capital diminishes financial fragility and "crowds out" deposits. The result of this fragile financial structure is that banks run the risk of losing funding if they attempt to withhold deposits. As such, the threat of bank runs exacerbates the problem that arises from withholding deposits. Consequently, by allowing banks to receive more deposits and extend more credit, financial fragility favors liquidity creation. As greater capital reduces financial fragility, it enhances the bargaining power of the bank and hampers the credibility of its commitment to the depositors. Thus, increased capital works to diminish liquidity creation.

Others argue that the opposite outcome is true. Higher capital ratios may create more liquidity because capital gives them an increased capacity to absorb the risks associated with liquidity creation. Specifically, the risk absorption hypothesis predicts that increased capital enhances the ability of banks to create liquidity. This hypothesis stems from two strands of the literature concerning the role of banks as risk transformers (refer to Figure 4.1 for the diagrammatic representation of this theory). Liquidity creation amplify banks' exposure to risk because banks that create more liquidity face greater losses when they are forced to sell illiquid assets to satisfy the liquidity demands of borrowers.[27,28] By contrast, more capital allows the bank to absorb greater risk.[29,30]

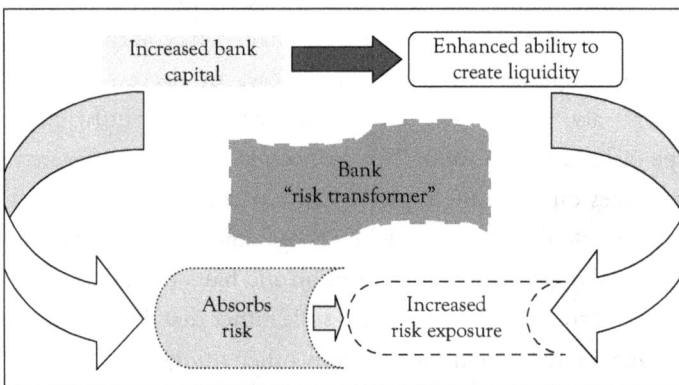

Figure 4.1 Flowchart: Risk absorption hypothesis
Source: Adapted from[31,32]

We agree with Berger and Bouwman[33] and others who propose that these two aforementioned hypotheses frame the causal link that moves from banks' capital to liquidity creation.

From the previously mentioned empirical studies and theoretical perspectives, it is evident that the relationship between capital and liquidity creation together with the impact of bank size is a highly topical problem that requires further study and clarification. In general, due to the array of methods, types of banks, bank sizes, and risk factors, the temptation to make substantial claims or assumptions are often tempered.

4.1.2 Basel III, Liquidity Creation and Bank Capital Data

We use 2002 to 2012 EMERG global liquidity data that consist of observations for LIBOR-based, insured banks.[34] In particular, we use databases consisting of individual banks' income statements as well as BS and OBS items.

The size differences among banks are significant and numerous empirical studies have indicated that components of liquidity creation vary greatly by bank size.[35–38] Therefore, we have categorized our data by bank size, with large banks' gross total assets (GTA) exceeding $3 billion, whereas medium banks have GTA ranging from $1 billion to $3 billion and small banks have GTA less than and equal to $1 billion.[39]

As in Chapter 3, a total of 391 hand-selected LIBOR-based banks from 38 countries were included in the study, including 157 large, 132 medium, and 102 small banks. These banks (with the number of large, medium and small banks in parenthesis for each jurisdiction, as well as * and ' denoting BCBS and MAG members, respectively) are located in Argentina* (1,1,2), Australia*' (5,1,1), Austria (2,3,2), Belgium* (1,1,1), Botswana (1,0,1), Brazil*' (3,1,0), Canada*' (7,2,1), China*' (7,1,0), Czech Republic (4,1,2), Finland (0,8,6), France*' (5,2,3), Germany*' (7,13,11), Hong Kong SAR* (1,7,1), Hungary (1,1,1), India* (6,4,2), Indonesia* (1,1,2), Ireland (3,1,0), Italy*' (2,7,4), Japan*' (14,2,3), Korea*' (6,3,1), Luxembourg* (0,1,0), Malta (0,1,2), Mexico*' (1,3,5), Namibia (0,1,0), the Netherlands*' (3,7,6), Norway (1,2,4), Poland (0,3,2), Portugal (3,1,2), Russia* (0,2,1), Saudi Arabia* (4,1,0), Singapore* (5,0,0), South Africa* (4,3,2), Spain*' (2,3,1), Sweden* (4,0,0),

Switzerland*' (3,4,1), Turkey* (7,1,0), United Kingdom*' (8,2,3), and United States*' (35,37,29).

The restrictions and computations associated with Basel III, liquidity creation, and bank capital are similar to that of Subsections 3.1.2.2 and 3.1.2.3, respectively.

4.1.3 Chapter 4: Main Contributions

The main contributions relating to Basel III, liquidity creation and bank capital are constituted by the answers to the questions listed as follows:

- **Question 4.1.1 (Liquidity Creation and Capital Data).** *How do we choose the control variables, viz., capital, credit risk, z-score, earnings volatility, nonperforming loans, size, market share, inflation, and unemployment, for liquidity creation and capital? (See Subsections 4.1.1, 4.1.2, and 4.4.1).*
- **Question 4.1.2 (Granger Causality Test for Liquidity Creation and Capital Variables).** *How does capital affect liquidity creation (narrow and broad measure) and vice versa in large, medium, and small banks? (See Table 4.10 and Subsections 4.2.4 and 4.3.2)*
- **Question 4.1.3 (Granger Causality Tests for Liquidity Creation, Capital and Control Variables for Large Banks).** *How does bank capital and liquidity creation (broad and narrow measure) affect all chosen control variables and vice versa in large banks? (See Table 4.11, 4.12, 4.13, and Subsections 4.2.4)*
- **Question 4.1.4 (Granger Causality Tests for Liquidity Creation, Capital and Control Variables for Medium Banks).** *How does bank capital and liquidity creation (broad and narrow measure) affect all the control variables and vice versa in medium banks? (See Table 4.14, 4.15, 4.16, and Subsections 4.2.4)*
- **Question 4.1.5 (Granger Causality Tests for Liquidity Creation, Capital and Control Variables for Small Banks).** *How does capital, liquidity creation (broad and narrow measure) affect all the control variables and vice versa in small banks? (See Table 4.17, 4.18, 4.19, and Subsections 4.2.4)*

- **Question 4.1.6 (Basel III Policy Implications for Liquidity Creation and Bank Capital).** *What are some of the Basel III policy implications that involve liquidity creation (broad and narrow measure) and capital for large, medium, and small banks? (See Subsection 4.3)*

4.2 Empirical Analysis of Liquidity Creation and Bank Capital

Our set of variables consists of (44 × 391) observations for the period 02Q1 to 12Q4. In the sequel, we highlight and interpret some pertinent observations of our aggregate data according to bank size (namely, large, medium, and small banks).

4.2.1 Descriptive Statistics of Liquidity Creation and Bank Capital Data

The descriptive statistics described in Tables 4.1, 4.2, and 4.3, involves the mean, maximum, minimum, standard deviation, skewness, kurtosis, Jarque-Bera, and probability of the Jarque-Bera statistics for EMERG data.

For large banks (see Table 4.1 for more details) *nonperforming loans, size, and unemployment* all display positive skewness close to zero. *Liquidity creation (broad and narrow measure), capital, and credit risk* exhibit negative skewness close to zero. The value of the kurtosis for *capital, credit risk, slightly* exceeds three, which means that the distribution is slightly peaked (leptokurtic) relative to the normal and exhibits some degree of leptokurtosis.[40] On the other hand, *liquidity creation (broad and narrow measure), nonperforming loans, size, and unemployment* exhibit kurtosis values of slightly less than three, which means that the distribution is slightly flat. The Jarque-Bera probability value is significant for *z-score, earnings volatility, market share, and inflation.*

For medium banks (see Table 4.2 for more details), *capital, credit risk, nonperforming loans, size, and unemployment,* all show positive skewness close to zero. *Liquidity creation (broad and narrow measure), z-score, earnings volatility, and market share* exhibit negative skewness close to

Table 4.1 Descriptive statistics of large banks

Variable	Mean	Max.	Min.	SD	Skewness	Kurtosis	JB	JB p-value
Liquidity creation: Broad measure	5.100289	5.680172	4.262680	0.400779	−0.542863	2.181597	3.389070	0.183685
Liquidity creation: Narrow measure	5.085711	5.631212	4.330733	0.385940	−0.556952	2.110709	3.724642	0.155312
Capital	−2.481834	−2.103734	−2.975930	0.187545	−0.480006	4.057616	3.740320	0.154099
Credit risk	−0.093674	0.191446	−0.452557	0.144079	−0.323960	3.479327	1.190850	0.551328
z-score	0.300629	1.701652	−4.509860	1.160105	−1.681016	7.788880	62.76714	0.000000*
Earnings volatility	0.102749	0.452843	0.002500	0.100447	1.927503	6.683858	52.12511	0.000000*
Nonperforming loans	2.202444	3.543362	1.162838	0.959349	0.286369	1.266662	6.109568	0.047133
Size	0.992893	1.071926	0.949339	0.034503	0.601956	2.221046	3.769648	0.151856
Market share	0.008091	0.012000	0.006000	0.001254	1.186777	4.313302	13.49063	0.001176*
Inflation	1.131431	1.840550	−0.963174	0.549626	−2.320461	9.083626	107.3392	0.000000*
Unemployment	1.858153	2.295896	1.489152	0.274550	0.334993	1.575461	4.543353	0.103139

Note: The table shows descriptive statistics (with the abbreviations max.: maximum; min.: minimum; SD: standard deviation; JB: Jarque-Bera; JB p-value: Jarque-Bera probability value; and obs.: observations) for large banks. *Significance: probability value p ≤ 0.05[41]

Table 4.2 Descriptive statistics of medium banks

Variable	Mean	Max.	Min.	SD	Skewness	Kurtosis	JB	JB *p*-value
Liquidity creation: Broad measure	2.533588	3.178054	1.098612	0.505647	-1.369576	4.471627	17.72584	0.000142*
Liquidity creation: Narrow measure	2.413782	3.178054	0.693147	0.706489	-1.169620	3.116121	10.05680	0.006549*
Capital	-2.170526	-1.838851	-2.441847	0.158388	0.608116	2.482722	3.202465	0.201648
Credit risk	-0.438707	-0.122168	-0.661649	0.126501	0.546735	2.684237	2.374868	0.305003
Z–score	0.712839	3.162094	-4.268698	1.459238	-0.762552	4.498971	8.383574	0.015119*
Earnings volatility	-3.088283	-0.512046	-5.298317	1.256348	-0.077442	1.935069	2.123122	0.345915
Nonperforming loans	0.786854	2.115532	-0.157824	0.890291	0.403099	1.434644	5.683871	0.058313
Size	0.726414	0.879627	0.571544	0.064575	0.179004	3.189325	0.300691	0.860411
Market share	-5.318202	-4.961845	-5.809143	0.206969	-0.737206	2.994196	3.985528	0.136318
Inflation	1.131431	1.840550	-0.963174	0.549626	-2.320461	9.083626	107.3392	0.000000*
Unemployment	1.858153	2.295896	1.489152	0.274550	0.334993	1.575461	4.543353	0.103139

Note: The table shows descriptive statistics (with the abbreviations max.: maximum; min.: minimum; SD: standard deviation; JB: Jarque-Bera; JB *p*-value: Jarque-Bera probability value; and obs.: observations) for medium banks. *Significance: probability value $p \leq 0.05$

Table 4.3 Descriptive statistics of small banks

Variable	Mean	Max.	Min.	SD	Skewness	Kurtosis	JB	JB p-value
Liquidity creation: Broad measure	0.442586	1.098612	-1.098612	0.657528	-1.121742	2.950770	9.232019	9.232019
Liquidity creation: Narrow measure	1.661235	2.484907	0.693147	0.570719	-0.172148	1.705918	3.287510	0.193253
Capital	-1.928371	-1.167962	-2.343407	0.332535	1.167262	3.165665	10.04198	0.006598*
Credit risk	-0.677270	0.170788	-0.933946	0.229509	1.031551	2.877259	7.830997	0.019931*
Z-score	1.070817	3.436018	-0.531028	1.145065	0.415879	1.863155	3.637773	0.162206
Earnings volatility	-2.998487	-1.592237	-7.110484	1.160257	-1.119845	4.635818	14.10221	0.000866*
Nonperforming loans	-0.303183	1.316944	-1.917323	1.135334	0.109282	1.425350	4.633371	0.098600
Size	0.451997	0.691145	0.040182	0.177379	-1.021785	3.028471	7.657816	0.021733*
Market share	-5.98114	-5.115996	-6.907755	0.549970	-0.689228	2.272924	4.452761	0.107918
Inflation	1.131431	1.840550	-0.963174	0.549626	-2.320461	9.083626	107.3392	0.000000*
Unemployment	1.858153	2.295896	1.489152	0.274550	0.334993	1.575461	4.543353	0.103139

Note: The table shows descriptive statistics (with the abbreviations max.: maximum; min.: minimum; SD: standard deviation; JB: Jarque–Bera; JB p-value: Jarque–Bera probability value; and obs.: observations) for small banks. *Significance: probability value $p \leq 0.05$

zero. The value of the kurtosis for *liquidity creation (broad and narrow measure) and size slightly* exceeds three, which implies that the distribution is slightly peaked (leptokurtic) relative to the normal and exhibits some degree of leptokurtosis. On the other hand, *capital, credit risk, earnings volatility, nonperforming loans, market share, and unemployment* exhibit kurtosis values of slightly less than three, which means that the distribution is slightly flat. The Jarque-Bera probability value is significant for *liquidity creation (broad and narrow measure), z-score, and inflation*. We accept the null hypothesis for normal distribution for *medium bank* variables, because our descriptive statistics is very close to the expected values for a normal distribution.

For small banks (see Table 4.3 for more details) *capital, credit risk, z-score, nonperforming loans, and unemployment* all show positive skewness close to zero. *Liquidity creation (broad and narrow measure), earnings volatility, size, and market share* exhibit negative skewness close to zero. The value of the kurtosis for *capital, earnings volatility, and size* slightly exceeds three, which means that the distribution is slightly peaked (leptokurtic) relative to the normal and exhibits some degree of leptokurtosis. On the other hand, *liquidity creation (broad and narrow measure), credit risk, z-score, nonperforming loans, market share and unemployment* exhibit kurtosis values of slightly less than three, which means that the distribution is slightly flat. The Jarque-Bera probability value is significant for *capital, credit risk, earnings volatility, size, and inflation*. We accept the null hypothesis for normal distribution for *small bank* variables, because our descriptive statistics is very close to the expected values for normal distribution.

4.2.2 Visual Inspection: Correlograms

In the ensuing section, we tabulate the results of the visual inspection of all the variables from the correlograms (refer to Tables 4.4, 4.5, and 4.6). Based on the correlograms for large banks (see Table 4.4), nine of the 11 variables became stationary after the first differencing.

Based on the correlograms for medium banks (refer to Table 4.5), eight of the 11 variables became stationary after the first differencing.

Table 4.4 *Correlogram summary for large banks*

Variables	Level/ 1st Diff.	AC	Q-Stat	Prob
Liquidity creation: Broad measure	Level	−0.209	211.38	0.000*
Liquidity creation: Broad measure	1st Diff.	−0.012	13.015	0.877
Liquidity creation: Narrow measure	Level	−0.158	61.873	0.000*
Liquidity creation: Narrow measure	1st Diff.	−0.013	9.6459	0.974
Capital	Level	0.040	162.32	0.000*
Capital	1st Diff.	−0.007	28.634	0.095
Credit risk	Level	−0.408	96.151	0.000*
Credit risk	1st Diff.	−0.078	23.497	0.265
Z-score	Level	−0.268	89.778	0.000*
Z-score	1st Diff.	−0.085	17.548	0.617
Earnings volatility	Level	−0.193	66.870	0.0000*
Earnings volatility	1st Diff.	−0.080	22.742	0.302
Nonperforming loans	Level	−0.351	272.14	0.000*
Nonperforming loans	1st Diff.	−0.021	70.462	0.000*
Size	Level	−0.248	165.76	0.000*
Size	1st Diff.	−0.019	26.613	0.147
Market share	Level	−0.158	61.873	0.0000*
Market share	1st Diff.	−0.056	10.948	0.948
Inflation	Level	−0.054	42.631	0.002*
Inflation	1st Diff.	0.032	22.555	0.311
Unemployment	Level	−0.364	268.98	0.000*
Unemployment	1st Diff.	−0.044	93.244	0.000*

Abbreviations: AC: autocorrelation coefficient; Q-stat: Q-statistic; prob: probability (null hypothesis) H_0: data is stationary; (alternative hypothesis) H_1: data is nonstationary p-value > 5%: accept the null; *p-value < 5%: reject the null

Table 4.5 Correlogram summary for medium banks

Variables	Level/ 1st Diff.	AC	Q-Stat	Prob
Liquidity creation: Broad measure	Level	−0.081	119.95	0.000*
Liquidity creation: Broad measure	1st Diff.	−0.152	37.427	0.010*
Liquidity creation: Narrow measure	Level	−0.103	155.43	0.000*
Liquidity creation: Narrow measure	1st Diff.	−0.094	18.451	0.558
Capital	Level	−0.386	220.02	0.000*
Capital	1st Diff.	0.059	18.669	0.543
Credit risk	Level	−0.342	148.60	0.000*
Credit risk	1st Diff.	0.009	11.729	0.925
Z-score	Level	−0.220	80.757	0.000*
Z-score	1st Diff.	0.061	20.678	0.416
Earnings volatility	Level	−0.308	81.422	0.000*
Earnings volatility	1st Diff.	−0.029	22.330	0.323
Nonperforming loans	Level	−0.363	285.96	0.000*
Nonperforming loans	1st Diff.	−0.147	139.53	0.000*
Size	Level	−0.037	65.527	0.000*
Size	1st Diff.	−0.211	14.788	0.788
Market share	Level	−0.182	111.52	0.000*
Market share	1st Diff.	−0.073	21.981	0.342
Inflation	Level	−0.054	42.631	0.002*
Inflation	1stDiff.	0.032	22.555	0.311
Unemployment	Level	−0.364	268.98	0.000*
Unemployment	1st Diff.	−0.044	93.244	0.000*

Abbreviations: AC: autocorrelation coefficient; Q-stat: Q-statistic; prob: probability (null hypothesis) H_o: data is stationary; (alternative hypothesis) H_1: data is nonstationary p-value > 5%: accept the null; *p-value < 5%: reject the null

Table 4.6 Correlogram summary for small banks

Variables	Level/ 1st Diff.	AC	Q-Stat	Prob
Liquidity creation: Broad measure	Level	−0.212	142.19	0.000*
Liquidity creation: Broad measure	1st Diff.	0.000	18.360	0.564
Liquidity creation: Narrow measure	Level	−0.232	259.67	0.000*
Liquidity creation: Narrow measure	1st Diff.	0.047	19.679	0.478
Capital	Level	0.061	40.888	0.004*
Capital	1st Diff.	0.147	17.735	0.605
Credit risk	Level	−0.114	130.48	0.000*
Credit risk	1st Diff.	0.114	46.099	0.001*
Z-score	Level	−0.243	165.80	0.000*
Z-score	1st Diff.	0.165	30.240	0.066
Earnings volatility	Level	−0.217	103.43	0.000*
Earnings volatility	1st Diff.	0.029	17.329	0.632
Nonperforming loans	Level	−0.304	279.56	0.000*
Nonperforming loans	1st Diff.	0.073	15.752	0.732
Size	Level	−0.087	126.99	0.000*
Size	1st Diff.	0.091	17.735	0.605
Market share	Level	0.023	43.623	0.002*
Market share	1st Diff.	−0.145	22.470	0.316
Inflation	Level	−0.054	42.631	0.002*
Inflation	1st Diff.	0.032	22.555	0.311
Unemployment	Level	−0.364	268.98	0.000*
Unemployment	1st Diff.	−0.044	93.244	0.000*

Abbreviations: AC: autocorrelation coefficient; *Q*-stat: *Q*-statistic; prob: probability (null hypothesis) H_o: data is stationary; (alternative hypothesis) H_1: data is nonstationary *p*-value > 5%: accept the null; **p*-value < 5%: reject the null

Based on the correlograms for small banks (see Table 4.6), nine of the 11 variables became stationary after first differencing.

4.2.3 Augmented Dickey Fuller (ADF) Results

The Augmented Dickey Fuller (ADF) statistic checks the stationarity of a series. In this regard, Tables 4.7 to 4.9, represent the results of the ADF test in large, medium, and small banks, respectively. This statistic, tests for the existence of a unit root in the level and first difference of each of the variables. The decision rule[42] for the aforementioned test is interesting. Table 4.7 records ADF results for large banks.

In particular, the ADF test results in Tables 4.7 to 4.9 consistently reveal that z-score and inflation for all three bank sizes are stationary at level. In general, for large, medium, and small banks, all other variables are nonstationary in their level form, and stationarity is obtained after first difference. This indicates that the series mainly contains one unit root and is of an integrated order one I(1) except for the z-score and inflation variables that are of integrated order zero for all bank sizes and denoted as I(0). The results of the ADF test confirm that our variables are stationary before further analysis.

4.2.4 Granger Causality Test Results

The Granger causality test determines whether the current and lagged value of one variable affects another. In this regard, Granger[43] postulated that a variable (X) Granger causes another variable (Y) if past and present values of X help to predict Y. The traditional Granger causality test uses F-test statistics and a probability value for causal relationships between variables. The ensuing tables show the results obtained when using the Granger causality test for large, medium, and small banks.

Our main causality test (see Table 4.10) involves bank capital and liquidity creation (for the *broad and narrow measures*) for large, medium, and small banks. For large banks, liquidity creation (narrow measure), Granger causes bank capital and vice versa at a 5% level of significance as shown by the F-statistics in Table 4.10. As such, we reject the null hypothesis and accept the alternative.

Table 4.7 *Records ADF results for large banks*

Variables	Level of test	Model	Number of lags	ADF test statistics	1% critical value	5% critical value	10% critical value	Prob.	Order of integration
Liquidity creation: Broad measure	Level	Constant	0	-2.153	-3.592	-2.931	-2.604	0.2258	
		Trend + Constant	0	-1.560	-4.186	-3.518	-3.190	0.7922	
		None	0	-2.408	-2.620	-1.949	-1.612	0.9954	
Liquidity creation: Broad measure	1st Diff.	Constant	0	-6.198	-3.597***	-2.933**	-2.605*	0.0000	I(1)
		Trend + Constant	0	-6.473	-4.192***	-3.521**	-3.191*	0.0000	I(1)
		None	0	-5.555	-2.621***	-1.949**	-1.612*	0.0000	I(1)
Liquidity creation: Narrow measure	Level	Constant	0	-1.928	-3.592	-2.931	-2.604	0.3166	
		Trend + Constant	0	-1.268	-4.186	-3.518	-3.190	0.8825	
		None	0	2.821	-2.620	-1.949	-1.612	0.9984	
Liquidity creation: Narrow measure	1st Diff.	Constant	0	-5.227	-3.597***	-2.93**	-2.605*	0.0001	I(1)
		Trend + Constant	0	-5.454	-4.192***	-3.521**	-3.192*	0.0003	I(1)
		None	0	-4.557	-2.621***	-1.949**	-1.612*	0.0000	I(1)
Capital	Level	Constant	1	-1.865	-3.597	-2.933	-2.605	0.3449	
		Trend + Constant	1	-1.861	-4.192	-3.521	-3.191	0.6567	
		None	1	-0.562	-2.621	-1.949	-1.612	0.4678	

Capital	1st Diff.	Constant	0	-3.903	-3.597***	-2.933**	-2.605*	0.0044	I(1)
		Trend + Constant	0	-3.875	-4.192	-3.521**	-3.191	0.0221	I(1)
		None	0	-3.918	-2.621***	-1.949**	-1.612*	0.0002	I(1)
Credit risk	Level	Constant	0	-2.879	-3.592	-2.931	-2.604	0.0562	
		Trend + Constant	0	-2.397	-4.187	-3.518	-3.190	0.3761	
		None	0	-2.707	-2.620***	-1.949**	-1.612*	0.0080	I(0)
Credit risk	1st Diff.	Constant	0	-7.483	-3.597***	-2.933**	-2.605*	0.0000	I(1)
		Trend + Constant	0	-7.847	-4.192***	-3.521**	-3.191*	0.0000	I(1)
		None	0	-7.527	-2.621***	-1.949**	-1.612*	0.0000	I(1)
Z-score	Level	Constant	0	-3.148	-3.593	-2.931**	-2.604*	0.0304	I(0)
		Trend + Constant	0	-3.426	-4.187	-3.518	-3.190	0.0612	
		None	0	-3.071	-2.620*	-1.949**	-1.612*	0.0029	I(0)
Z-score	1st Diff.	Constant	1	-6.957	-3.601***	-2.935**	-2.606*	0.0000	I(1)
		Trend + Constant	1	-6.933	-4.199***	-3.524**	-3.193	0.0000	I(1)
		None	1	-7.055	-2.623***	-1.949**	-1.612*	0.0000	I(1)
Earnings volatility	Level	Constant	1	-2.846	-3.597	-2.933	-2.605	0.0605	
		Trend + Constant	1	-2.858	-4.192	-3.521	-3.192	0.1860	
		None	1	-1.869	-2.621	-1.949	-1.612	0.0594	
Earnings volatility	1st Diff.	Constant	2	-4.686	-3.606***	-2.937**	-2.607*	0.0005	I(1)
		Trend + Constant	2	-4.642	-4.205***	-3.527**	-3.197*	0.0032	I(1)

(Continued)

Table 4.7 (Continued)

Variables	Level of test	Model	Number of lags	ADF test statistics	1% critical value	5% critical value	10% critical value	Prob.	Order of integration
Nonperforming loans	Level	None	2	-4.757	-2.624***	-1.949**	-1.612*	0.0000	I(1)
		Constant	1	-0.910	-3.597	-2.933	-2.605	0.7753	
		Trend + Constant	1	-1.730	-4.192	-3.521	-3.191	0.7202	
		None	1	0.566	-2.621	-1.949	-1.612	0.8346	
Nonperforming loans	1st Diff.	Constant	0	-3.551	-3.597	-2.933**	-2.605*	0.0113	I(1)
		Trend + Constant	0	-3.503	-4.192	-3.521	-3.191	0.0520	
		None	0	-3.392	-2.621***	-1.949**	-1.612*	0.0012	I(1)
Size	Level	Constant	1	-0.943	-3.597	-2.933	-2.605	0.7643	
		Trend + Constant	1	-2.975	-4.192	-3.521	-3.191	0.1510	
		None	1	0.984	-2.621	-1.949	-1.612	0.9113	
Size	1st Diff.	Constant	0	-4.473	-3.597***	-2.933**	-2.605*	0.0009	I(1)
		Trend + Constant	0	-4.462	-4.192***	-3.521**	-3.191*	0.0049	I(1)
		None	0	-4.355	-2.621***	-1.949**	-1.612*	0.0001	I(1)
Market share	Level	Constant	0	-3.054	-3.593	-2.931**	-2.604**	0.0379	I(0)
		Trend + Constant	0	-2.943	-4.187	-3.518	-3.190	0.1599	
		None	0	-0.284	-2.620	-1.949	-1.612	0.5778	

Market share	1st Diff.	Constant	0	-7.610	-3.597***	-2.933**	-2.605*	0.0000	I(1)
		Trend + Constant	0	-7.610	-4.192***	-3.521**	-3.191*	0.0000	I(1)
		None	0	-7.703	-2.621***	-1.949**	-1.612*	0.0000	I(1)
Inflation	Level	Constant	1	-3.927	-3.597***	-2.933**	-2.605*	0.0041	I(0)
		Trend + Constant	1	-3.980	-4.192	-3.521**	-3.191*	0.0171	I(0)
		None	1	-1.348	-2.621	-1.949	-1.612	0.1619	
Inflation	1st Diff.	Constant	0	-4.762	-3.597***	-2.933**	-2.605*	0.0004	I(1)
		Trend + Constant	0	-4.705	-4.192***	-3.521**	-3.191*	0.0025	I(1)
		None	0	-4.820	-2.621***	-1.949**	-1.612*	0.0000	I(1)
Unemployment	Level	Constant	1	-1.258	-3.597	-2.933	-2.605	0.6401	
		Trend + Constant	1	-1.914	-4.192	-3.521	-3.191	0.6297	
		None	1	0.106	-2.621	-1.949	-1.612	0.7108	
Unemployment	1st Diff.	Constant	0	-3.099	-3.597	-2.933**	-2.605*	0.0342	I(1)
		Trend + Constant	0	-3.065	-4.192	-3.521	-3.191	0.1278	
		None	0	-3.125	-2.621***	-1.949**	-1.612*	0.0025	I(1)

Note:

Prob. (Probability): 5% significance level (reject null hypothesis (nonstationary) and accept alternative hypothesis (stationary) when *p*-values < 5%, MacKinnon (1996) one–sided *p*-values.

I(0) indicates no unit root in levels and is stationary at level.

I(1) indicates unit root in levels and is stationary after first differencing.

Reject null hypothesis (nonstationary) when test critical values are: *** 1%, ** 5%, *10% significant.

Table 4.8 Records ADF results for medium banks

Variables	Level of test	Model	Number of lags	ADF test statistics	1% critical value	5% critical value	10% critical value	Prob.#	Order of integration
Liquidity creation: Broad measure	Level	Constant	2	-2.386	-3.601	-2.935	-2.606	0.1518	
		Trend + Constant	2	-3.760	-4.199	-3.524**	-3.193*	0.0292	I(0)
		None	2	0.857	-2.623	-1.949	-1.612	0.8914	
Liquidity creation: Broad measure	1st Diff.	Constant	1	-2.835	-3.601	-2.935	-2.606	0.0622	
		Trend + Constant	1	-2.638	-4.199	-3.524	-3.193	0.2667	I(1)
		None	1	-2.718	-2.623***	-1.949**	-1.612*	0.0078	
Liquidity creation: Narrow measure	Level	Constant	0	-3.398	-3.593	-2.931**	-2.604*	0.0165	I(0)
		Trend + Constant	0	-1.995	-4.187	-3.518	-3.190	0.5875	
		None	6	0.383	-2.629	-1.950	-1.611	0.7895	
Liquidity creation: Narrow measure	1st Diff.	Constant	0	-5.508	-3.597***	-2.933**	-2.605*	0.0000	I(1)
		Trend + Constant	0	-6.545	-4.192***	-3.521**	-3.191*	0.0000	I(1)
		None	0	-4.436	-2.621***	-1.949**	-1.612*	0.0000	I(1)
Capital	Level	Constant	0	-1.578	-3.593	-2.931	-2.604	0.4852	
		Trend + Constant	0	-1.038	-4.187	-3.518	-3.190	0.9276	
		None	0	-0.369	-2.620	-1.949	-1.612	0.5457	

Capital	1st Diff.	Constant	1	-4.916	-3.601***	-2.935**	-2.606*	0.0002	I(1)
		Trend + Constant	0	-6.830	-4.192***	-3.521**	-3.191*	0.0000	I(1)
		None	1	-4.982	-2.623***	-1.949**	-1.612*	0.0000	I(1)
Credit risk	Level	Constant	0	-2.147	-3.593	-2.931	-2.604	0.2282	
		Trend + Constant	0	-1.911	-4.187	-3.518	-3.190	0.6318	
		None	0	-0.812	-2.620	-1.949	-1.612	0.3583	
Credit risk	1st Diff.	Constant	0	-7.360	-3.597***	-2.933**	-2.605*	0.0000	I(1)
		Trend + Constant	0	-7.291	-4.192***	-3.521**	-3.191*	0.0000	I(1)
		None	0	-7.463	-2.621***	-1.949**	-1.612*	0.0000	I(1)
Z–score	Level	Constant	0	-3.150	-3.592	-2.931	-2.604*	0.0302	I(0)
		Trend + Constant	0	-4.367	-4.187***	-3.518**	-3.190*	0.0062	I(0)
		None	0	-2.887	-2.620***	-1.949**	-1.612*	0.0049	I(0)
Z–score	1st Diff.	Constant	0	-9.028	-3.597***	-2.933**	-2.605*	0.0000	I(1)
		Trend + Constant	0	-8.915	-4.192***	-3.521**	-3.191*	0.0000	I(1)
		None	0	-9.112	-2.621***	-1.949**	-1.612*	0.0000	I(1)
Earnings volatility	Level	Constant	0	-3.043	-3.593	-2.931	-2.604*	0.0388	I(0)
		Trend + Constant	0	-4.380	-4.187***	-3.518**	-3.190*	0.0060	I(0)
		None	1	-1.074	-2.621	-1.949	-1.612	0.2515	

(Continued)

Table 4.8 (Continued)

Variables	Level of test	Model	Number of lags	ADF test statistics	1% critical value	5% critical value	10% critical value	Prob.#	Order of integration
Earnings volatility	1st Diff.	Constant	0	-10.258	-3.597***	-2.933**	-2.605*	0.0000	I(1)
		Trend + Constant	0	-10.112	-4.192***	-3.521**	-3.191*	0.0000	I(1)
		None	0	-10.353	-2.621***	-1.949**	-1.612*	0.0000	I(1)
Nonperforming loans	Level	Constant	1	-0.563	-3.597	-2.933	-2.605	0.8680	
		Trend + Constant	2	-2.414	-4.199	-3.524	-3.193	0.3671	
		None	1	0.299	-2.621	-1.949	-1.612	0.7677	
Nonperforming loans	1st Diff.	Constant	0	-2.945	-3.597	-2.933**	-2.605*	0.0487	I(1)
		Trend + Constant	0	-2.887	-4.192	-3.521	-3.191	0.1770	
		None	0	-2.595	-2.621	-1.949**	-1.612*	0.0107	I(1)
Size	Level	Constant	0	-2.106	-3.593	-2.931	-2.604	0.2433	
		Trend + Constant	0	-2.934	-4.187	-3.518	-3.190	0.1626	
		None	0	0.810	-2.620	-1.949	-1.612	0.8834	
Size	1st Diff.	Constant	0	-8.250	-3.597***	-2.933**	-2.605*	0.0000	I(1)
		Trend + Constant	0	-8.170	-4.192***	-3.521**	-3.191*	0.0000	I(1)
		None	0	-8.051	-2.621***	-1.949**	-1.612*	0.0000	I(1)

Market share	Level	Constant	0	−2.477	−3.593	−2.931	−2.604	0.1280	
		Trend + Constant	0	−2.447	−4.187	−3.518	−3.190	0.3518	
		None	0	−0.504	−2.620	−1.949	−1.612	0.4921	
Market share	1st Diff.	Constant	0	−8.255	−3.597***	−2.933**	−2.605*	0.0000	I(1)
		Trend + Constant	0	−8.151	−4.192***	−3.521**	−3.191*	0.0000	I(1)
		None	0	−8.311	−2.621***	−1.949**	−1.612*	0.0000	I(1)
Inflation	Level	Constant	1	−3.927	−3.597***	−2.933**	−2.605***	0.0041	I(0)
		Trend + Constant	1	−3.980	−4.192	−3.521**	−3.191*	0.0171	I(0)
		None	1	−1.348	−2.621	−1.949	−1.612	0.1619	
Inflation	1st Diff.	Constant	0	−4.762	−3.597***	−2.933**	−2.605*	0.0004	I(1)
		Trend + Constant	0	−4.705	−4.192***	−3.521**	−3.191*	0.0025	I(1)
		None	0	−4.820	−2.621***	−1.949**	−1.612*	0.0000	I(1)
Unemployment	Level	Constant	1	−1.258	−3.597	−2.933	−2.605	0.6401	
		Trend + Constant	1	−1.914	−4.192	−3.521	−3.191	0.6297	
		None	1	0.106	−2.621	−1.949	−1.612	0.7108	

(Continued)

Table 4.8 (Continued)

Variables	Level of test	Model	Number of lags	ADF test statistics	1% critical value	5% critical value	10% critical value	Prob.#	Order of integration
Unemployment	1st Diff.	Constant	0	–3.099	–3.597	–2.933**	–2.605*	0.0342	I(1)
		Trend + Constant	0	–3.065	–4.192	–3.521	–3.191	0.1278	
		None	0	–3.125	–2.621***	–1.949**	–1.612*	0.0025	I(1)

Note:

Prob. (Probability): 5% significance level (reject null hypothesis (nonstationary) and accept alternative hypothesis (stationary) when *p*-values < 5%, MacKinnon (1996) one–sided *p*-values.

I(0) indicates no unit root in levels and is stationary at level.

I(1) indicates unit root in levels and is stationary after first differencing.

Reject null hypothesis (nonstationary) when test critical values are: *** 1%, ** 5%, *10% significant.

Table 4.9 Records ADF results for small banks

Variables	Level of test	Model	Number of lags	ADF test statistics	1% critical value	5% critical value	10% critical value	Prob.#	Order of integration
Liquidity creation: Broad measure	Level	Constant	0	-1.383	-3.593	-2.931	-2.604	0.5816	
		Trend + Constant	0	-0.815	-4.187	-3.518	-3.190	0.9561	
		None	0	-1.162	-2.620	-1.949	-1.612	0.2201	
Liquidity creation: Broad measure	1st Diff.	Constant	0	-6.325	-3.597***	-2.933**	-2.605*	0.0000	I(1)
		Trend + Constant	0	-6.523	-4.192***	-3.521**	-3.191*	0.0000	I(1)
		None	0	-6.403	-2.621***	-1.949**	-1.612*	0.0000	I(1)
Liquidity creation: Narrow measure	Level	Constant	2	-0.094	-3.601	-2.935	-2.606	0.9433	
		Trend + Constant	0	-3.307	-4.186	-3.518	-3.190	0.0787	
		None	0	-1.702	-2.620	-1.949	-1.612	0.9768	
Liquidity creation: Narrow measure	1st Diff.	Constant	1	-4.990	-3.601***	-2.935**	-2.606*	0.0002	I(1)
		Trend + Constant	1	-4.984	-4.199***	-3.524**	-3.193*	0.0012	I(1)
		None	7	-0.536	-2.633	-1.951	-1.611	0.4778	
Capital	Level	Constant	3	-1.602	-3.606	-2.937	-2.607	0.4722	
		Trend + Constant	1	-5.712	-4.192***	-3.521**	-3.191*	0.0001	I(0)
		None	3	0.708	-2.624	-1.949	-1.612	0.8641	

(Continued)

Table 4.9 (Continued)

Variables	Level of test	Model	Number of lags	ADF test statistics	1% critical value	5% critical value	10% critical value	Prob.#	Order of integration
Capital	1st Diff.	Constant	1	-7.120	-3.601***	-2.935**	-2.606*	0.0000	I(1)
		Trend + Constant	1	-6.937	-4.199***	-3.524**	-3.193*	0.0000	I(1)
		None	1	-7.149	-2.623***	-1.949**	-1.612*	0.0000	I(1)
Credit risk	Level	Constant	5	-2.803	-3.616	-2.941	-2.609*	0.0673	
		Trend + Constant	5	-0.931	-4.219	-3.533	-3.198	0.9417	
		None	3	0.914	-2.624	-1.949	-1.612	0.9005	
Credit risk	1st Diff.	Constant	2	-7.282	-3.606***	-2.937**	-2.607*	0.0000	I(1
		Trend + Constant	2	-7.429	-4.205***	-3.527**	-3.195*	0.0000	I(1)
		None	1	-8.303	-2.623***	-1.949**	-1.612*	0.0000	I(1)
z-score	Level	Constant	0	-1.614	-3.593	-2.931	-2.604	0.4670	
		Trend + Constant	8	-4.886	-4.244***	-3.544**	-3.205*	0.0020	I(0)
		None	0	-1.653	-2.620	-1.949	-1.612	0.0923	
z-score	1st Diff.	Constant	0	-7.917	-3.597***	-2.933**	-2.605*	0.0000	I(1)
		Trend + Constant	0	-7.884	-4.192***	-3.521**	-3.191*	0.0000	I(1)
		None	0	-7.973	-2.621***	-1.949**	-1.612*	0.0000	I(1)

Earnings volatility	Level	Constant	0	-2.744	-3.593	-2.931	-2.604	0.0751	
		Trend + Constant	0	-3.549	-4.187	-3.518**	-3.190*	0.0466	I(0)
		None	0	-1.341	-2.620	-1.949	-1.612	0.1640	
Earnings volatility	1st Diff.	Constant	0	-9.204	-3.597	-2.933	-2.605	0.0000	I(1)
		Trend + Constant	0	-9.095	-4.192	-3.521	-3.191	0.0000	I(1)
		None	0	-9.295	-2.621	-1.949	-1.612	0.0000	I(1)
Nonperforming loans	Level	Constant	0	-0.223	-3.593	-2.931	-2.604	0.9275	
		Trend + Constant	8	-3.016	-4.244	-3.544	-3.205	0.1425	
		None	0	-0.661	-2.620	-1.949	-1.612	0.4249	
Nonperforming loans	1st Diff.	Constant	1	-6.449	-3.601***	-2.935**	-2.606*	0.0000	I(1)
		Trend + Constant	1	-6.295	-4.199***	-3.524**	-3.193*	0.0000	I(1)
		None	5	-1.570	-2.629	-1.950	-1.612	0.1081	
Size	Level	Constant	3	-1.533	-3.606	-2.937	-2.607	0.5071	
		Trend + Constant	3	-1.776	-4.205	-3.527	-3.195	0.6975	
		None	3	-1.344	-2.624	-1.949	-1.612	0.9526	
Size	1st Diff.	Constant	1	-6.592	-3.601***	-2.935**	-2.606*	0.0000	I(1)
		Trend + Constant	1	-6.511	-4.199***	-3.524**	-3.193*	0.0000	I(1)
		None	5	-2.517	-2.629	-1.950**	-1.611*	0.0133	I(1)

(Continued)

Table 4.9 (Continued)

Variables	Level of test	Model	Number of lags	ADF test statistics	1% critical value	5% critical value	10% critical value	Prob.#	Order of integration
Market share	Level	Constant	0	-3.251	-3.592	-2.931**	-2.604*	0.0237	I(0)
		Trend + Constant	0	-4.872	-4.187***	-3.518***	-3.190*	0.0016	I(0)
		None	3	-1.257	-2.624	-1.949	-1.612	0.1887	
Market share	1st Diff.	Constant	1	-7.227	-3.601****	-2.935**	-2.606*	0.0000	I(1)
		Trend + Constant	1	-7.127	-4.199****	-3.524**	-3.193*	0.0000	I(1)
		None	1	-7.210	-2.623****	-1.949**	-1.612*	0.0000	I(1)
Inflation	Level	Constant	1	-3.927	-3.597****	-2.933**	-2.605*	0.0041	I(0)
		Trend + Constant	1	-3.980	-4.192	-3.521**	-3.191*	0.0171	I(0)
		None	1	-1.348	-2.621	-1.949	-1.612	0.1619	
Inflation	1st Diff.	Constant	0	-4.762	-3.597****	-2.933**	-2.605*	0.0004	I(1)
		Trend + Constant	0	-4.705	-4.192***	-3.521**	-3.191*	0.0025	I(1)
		None	0	-4.820	-2.621***	-1.949**	-1.612*	0.0000	I(1)

Unemployment	Level	Constant	1	-1.258	-3.597	-2.933	-2.605	0.6401	
		Trend + Constant	1	-1.914	-4.192	-3.521	-3.191	0.6297	
		None	1	0.106	-2.621	-1.949	-1.612	0.7108	
Unemployment	1st Diff.	Constant	0	-3.099	-3.597	-2.933**	-2.605*	0.0342	I(1)
		Trend + Constant	0	-3.065	-4.192	-3.521	-3.191	0.1278	
		None	0	-3.125	-2.621***	-1.949**	-1.612*	0.0025	I(1)

Note:
Prob. (Probability): 5% significance level (reject null hypothesis (nonstationary) and accept alternative hypothesis (stationary) when p-values $<$ 5%, MacKinnon (1996) one–sided p-values.
I(0) indicates no unit root in levels and is stationary at level.
I(1) indicates unit root in levels and is stationary after first differencing.
Reject null hypothesis (nonstationary) when test critical values are: *** 1%, ** 5%, *10% significant.

Table 4.10 *Granger causality test*

	Broad measure				Narrow measure			
	Null hypothesis	Obs	F-statistics	Prob	Null hypothesis	Obs	F-statistics	Prob
Large banks	LCBM does not Granger cause BC	41	0.18761	0.8297	LCNM does not Granger cause BC	41	3.22257	0.0516**
	BC does not Granger cause LCBM		0.39999	0.6733	BC does not Granger cause LCNM		4.00370	0.0269**
Medium banks	LCBM does not Granger cause BC	41	2.38764	0.1062	LCNM does not Granger cause BC	41	2.98595	0.0631*
	BC does not Granger cause LCBM		5.02276	0.0119**	BC does not Granger cause LCNM		2.54020	0.0929*
Small banks	LCBM does not Granger cause BC	41	0.16983	0.8445	LCNM does not Granger cause BC	41	1.69378	0.1981
	BC does not Granger cause LCBM		2.51001	0.0954*	BC does not Granger cause LCNM		3.14014	0.0553*

Abbreviations: LCBM: liquidity creation broad measure; LCNM: liquidity creation narrow measure; BC: bank capital
**5% level of significance
*10% level of significance

For medium banks, capital Granger causes liquidity creation (broad measure) at a 5% level of significance. Furthermore, a bidirectional causal relationship exists between capital and liquidity creation (narrow measure) at a 10% level of significance.

For small banks, capital Granger causes liquidity creation (broad and narrow measure) at a 10% level of significance.

Table 4.11 displays results of the causality test that involves liquidity creation (*broad measure*) and all the control variables. For large banks, earnings volatility as well as inflation Granger causes liquidity creation (broad measure) at a 5% level of significance. As such, we reject the null hypothesis and accept the alternative. This result implies that for large banks, changes to earnings volatility and inflation affect liquidity creation. The causality is unidirectional, from earnings volatility and inflation to liquidity creation (broad measure).

Table 4.12 displays the outcomes of the causality test that involves liquidity creation (*narrow measure*) and all the control variables. For large banks, *bank size* has a bidirectional causal relationship with *liquidity creation* (*narrow measure*) at a 5% level of significance. Furthermore, *inflation* has a unidirectional causal relationship with liquidity creation (*narrow measure*) at a 5% level of significance.

Table 4.13 shows the outcomes of the causality test that involves bank capital and all the control variables. For large banks, *earnings volatility* Granger causes bank capital at a 5% level of significance. Also, *capital* Granger causes *bank size* for large banks at a 10% level of significance. In addition, a bidirectional causal relationship exists between inflation and bank capital at a 10% and 5% level of significance.

Table 4.14 shows the results of the causality test that involves liquidity creation (broad measure) and all the control variables for medium banks. *Credit risk* Granger causes *liquidity creation* (*broad measure*) at a 5% level of significance. In addition, *liquidity creation* (*broad measure*) Granger causes *bank size* at a 10% level of significance.

Table 4.15 exhibits the outcomes of the causality test that involves liquidity creation (narrow measure) and all the control variables for medium banks. *z-score* Granger causes *liquidity creation* (*narrow measure*) at a 10% level of significance. Additionally, *nonperforming loans* Granger causes *liquidity creation* (*narrow measure*) at a 5% level of significance.

Table 4.11 Granger causality test for large banks (broad measure)

Null hypothesis	No. of observations	F-Statistics	Probability	Conclusion
DCR does not Granger cause DLCBM	41	0.97831	0.3857	No causality
DLCBM does not Granger cause DCR		1.10418	0.3424	No causality
Zscore does not Granger cause DLCBM	41	0.52494	0.5960	No causality
DLCBM does not Granger cause zscore		1.48079	0.2410	No causality
DEV does not Granger cause DLCBM	41	4.30059	0.0211**	Causality
DLCBM does not Granger cause DEV		2.13617	0.1328	No causality
DNPL does not Granger cause DLCBM	41	0.36828	0.6945	No causality
DLCBM does not Granger cause DNPL		0.04759	0.9536	No causality
DBS does not Granger cause DLCBM	41	0.24421	0.7846	No causality
DLCBM does not Granger cause DBS		0.58444	0.5626	No causality
DMS does not Granger cause DLCBM	41	0.87066	0.4273	No causality
DLCBM does not Granger cause DMS		0.89892	0.4159	No causality
INF does not Granger cause DLCBM	41	6.78940	0.0031**	Causality
DLCBM does not Granger cause INF		1.99616	0.1506	No causality
DUR does not Granger cause DLCBM	41	0.43179	0.6527	No causality
DLCBM does not Granger cause DUR		1.82541	0.1758	No causality

Abbreviations: DCR: differenced credit risk; DLCBM: differenced liquidity creation broad measure; DEV: differenced earnings volatility; DNPL: differenced nonperforming loans; DBS: differenced bank size; INF: inflation; DUR: differenced unemployment rates
**5% level of significance
*10% level of significance

Table 4.12 Granger causality test for large banks (narrow measure)

Null hypothesis	No. of observations	F-statistics	Probability	Conclusion
DCR does not Granger cause DLCNM	41	0.62912	0.5388	No causality
DLCNM does not Granger cause DCR		1.98712	0.1518	No causality
ZSCORE does not Granger cause DLCNM	41	0.33357	0.7186	No causality
DLCNM does not Granger cause ZSCORE		0.00418	0.9958	No causality
DEV does not Granger cause DLCNM	41	1.12926	0.3345	No causality
DLCNM does not Granger cause DEV		0.12484	0.8830	No causality
DNPL does not Granger cause DLCNM	41	2.21765	0.1235	No causality
DLCNM does not Granger cause DNPL		1.39599	0.2607	No causality
DBS does not Granger cause DLCNM	41	8.53173	0.0009**	Causality
DLCNM does not Granger cause DBS		5.15462	0.0108**	Causality
DMS does not Granger cause DLCNM	41	1.73853	0.1902	No causality
DLCNM does not Granger cause DMS		0.85840	0.4323	No causality
INF does not Granger cause DLCNM	41	4.27975	0.0215**	Causality
DLCNM does not Granger cause INF		1.52243	0.2319	No causality
DUR does not Granger cause DLCNM	41	0.29504	0.7463	No causality
DLCNM does not Granger cause DUR		1.22992	0.3043	No causality

Abbreviations: DCR: differenced credit risk; DLCNM: differenced liquidity creation narrow measure; DEV: differenced earnings volatility; DNPL: differenced nonperforming loans; DBS: differenced bank size; INF: inflation; DUR: differenced unemployment rates
**5% level of significance
*10% level of significance

Table 4.13 Granger causality test for large banks (capital)

Null hypothesis	No. of observations	F-statistics	Probability	Conclusion
DCR does not Granger cause DBC	41	0.10158	0.9037	No causality
DBC does not Granger cause DCR		0.42062	0.6598	No causality
Zscore does not Granger cause DBC	41	0.47210	0.6275	No causality
DBC does not Granger cause zscore		0.03179	0.9687	No causality
DEV does not Granger cause DBC	41	4.08581	0.0252**	Causality
DBC does not Granger cause DEV		1.73745	0.1904	No causality
DNPL does not Granger cause DBC	41	1.33509	0.2759	No causality
DBC does not Granger cause DNPL		1.12920	0.3345	No causality
DBS does not Granger cause DBC	41	1.63703	0.2087	No causality
DBC does not Granger cause DBS		2.81772	0.0730*	Causality
DMS does not Granger cause DBC	41	0.90029	0.4154	No causality
DBC does not Granger cause DMS		0.68428	0.5109	No causality
INF does not Granger cause DBC	41	3.10022	0.0572*	Causality
DBC does not Granger cause INF		3.85630	0.0304**	Causality
DUR does not Granger cause DBC	41	0.99499	0.3797	No causality
DBC does not Granger cause DUR		1.82845	0.1753	No causality

Abbreviations: DCR: differenced credit risk; DBC: differenced bank capital; DEV: differenced earnings volatility; DNPL: differenced nonperforming loans; DBS: differenced bank size; INF: inflation; DUR: differenced unemployment rates
**5% level of significance
*10% level of significance

Table 4.14 Granger causality test for medium banks (liquidity creation: broad measure)

Null hypothesis	No. of observations	F-statistics	Probability	Conclusion
DCR does not Granger cause DLCBM	41	4.01863	0.0266**	Causality
DLCBM does not Granger cause DCR		0.26736	0.7669	No causality
Zscore does not Granger cause DLCBM	41	1.01318	0.3732	No causality
DLCBM does not Granger cause zscore		0.89137	0.4190	No causality
DEV does not Granger cause DLCBM	41	0.55509	0.5789	No causality
DLCBM does not Granger cause DEV		0.44733	0.6428	No causality
DNPL does not Granger cause DLCBM	41	0.61417	0.5467	No causality
DLCBM does not Granger cause DNPL		1.51828	0.2328	No causality
DBS does not Granger cause DLCBM	41	0.45421	0.6385	No causality
DLCBM does not Granger cause DBS		2.81025	0.0734*	Causality
DMS does not Granger cause DLCBM	41	0.06113	0.9408	No causality
DLCBM does not Granger cause DMS		1.37496	0.2658	No causality
INF does not Granger cause DLCBM	41	1.53840	0.2285	No causality
DLCBM does not Granger cause INF		0.32108	0.7274	No causality
DUR does not Granger cause DLCBM	41	0.86475	0.4297	No causality
DLCBM does not Granger cause DUR		0.74676	0.4811	No causality

Abbreviations: DCR: differenced credit risk; DLCBM: differenced liquidity creation broad measure; DEV: differenced earnings volatility; DNPL: differenced nonperforming loans; DBS: differenced bank size; INF: inflation; DUR: differenced unemployment rates
**5% level of significance
*10% level of significance

Table 4.15 Granger causality test for medium banks (liquidity creation: narrow measure)

Null hypothesis	No. of observations	F-statistics	Probability	Conclusion
DCR does not Granger cause DLCNM	41	0.18519	0.8317	No causality
DLCNM does not Granger cause DCR		0.79275	0.4603	No causality
Zscore does not Granger cause DLCNM	41	2.75510	0.0770*	Causality
DLCNM does not Granger cause zscore		0.65826	0.5239	No causality
DEV does not Granger cause DLCNM	41	0.07282	0.9299	No causality
DLCNM does not Granger cause DEV		0.02305	0.9772	No causality
DNPL does not Granger cause DLCNM	41	3.26560	0.0497**	Causality
DLCNM does not Granger cause DNPL		0.74049	0.4840	No causality
DBS does not Granger cause DLCNM	41	0.09393	0.9106	No causality
DLCNM does not Granger cause DBS		0.99118	0.3810	No causality
DMS does not Granger cause DLCNM	41	0.20593	0.8148	No causality
DLCNM does not Granger cause DMS		1.00184	0.3772	No causality
INF does not Granger cause DLCNM	41	2.06150	0.1420	No causality
DLCNM does not Granger cause INF		0.56866	0.5713	No causality
DUR does not Granger cause DLCNM	41	1.82436	0.1759	No causality
DLCNM does not Granger cause DUR		2.39153	0.1059	No causality

Abbreviations: DCR: differenced credit risk; DLCNM: differenced liquidity creation narrow measure; DEV: differenced earnings volatility; DNPL: differenced nonperforming loans; DBS: differenced bank size; INF: inflation; DUR: differenced unemployment rates
**5% level of significance
*10% level of significance

Table 4.16 shows the results of the causality test that involves bank capital and all the control variables for medium banks. *Bank capital* Granger causes *bank size (10% sig.), market share (10% sig.), and unemployment (5% sig.)*, respectively. Additionally, *inflation* Granger causes *bank capital* at a 5% level of significance.

Table 4.17 shows the results of the causality test that involves liquidity creation (broad measure) and all the control variables for small banks. *Credit risk, nonperforming loans, and market share* Granger causes liquidity creation (broad measure) at a 5% level of significance. On the other hand, liquidity creation (broad measure) Granger causes *inflation* for small banks at a 5% level of significance.

Table 4.18 shows the results of the causality test that involves liquidity creation (narrow measure) and all the control variables for small banks. Only liquidity creation (narrow measure) Granger causes market share at a 10% level of significance.

Table 4.19 shows the results of the causality test that involves bank capital and all the control variables for small banks. *Credit risk* Granger causes bank capital at a 10% level of significance. Also, bank capital Granger causes *z*-score at a 10% level of significance. In addition, earnings volatility and capital has a bidirectional causal relationship for small banks at a 10% level of significance. Furthermore, bank capital Granger causes market share for small banks at a 5% level of significance.

4.3 Implications of Liquidity Creation and Bank Capital

In this section, we draw the most important conclusions arrived at in our analysis in preceding sections.

4.3.1 Implications (Liquidity Creation and Bank Capital Data)

We are able to draw conclusions about liquidity creation and capital data as alluded to in Question 4.1.1 of Subsection 4.1.3. A total of 391 banks from 38 countries were included in the study and then subdivided into large, medium and small banks based on the level of GTA.

Table 4.16 Granger causality test for medium banks (capital)

Null hypothesis	No. of observations	F-statistics	Probability	Conclusion
DCR does not Granger cause DBC	41	0.83714	0.4412	No causality
DBC does not Granger cause DCR		12.6129	7.E-05	No causality
Zscore does not Granger cause DBC	41	1.62304	0.2114	No causality
DBC does not Granger cause zscore		1.37418	0.2660	No causality
DEV does not Granger cause DBC	41	1.33006	0.2771	No causality
DBC does not Granger cause DEV		1.10011	0.3438	No causality
DNPL does not Granger cause DBC	41	0.39158	0.6788	No causality
DBC does not Granger cause DNPL		0.17980	0.8362	No causality
DBS does not Granger cause DBC	41	0.64513	0.5306	No causality
DBC does not Granger cause DBS		2.46731	0.0990*	Causality
DMS does not Granger cause DBC	41	0.10449	0.9011	No causality
DBC does not Granger cause DMS		2.91384	0.0672*	Causality
INF does not Granger cause DBC	41	5.74855	0.0068**	Causality
DBC does not Granger cause INF		0.26849	0.7661	No causality
DUR does not Granger cause DBC	41	0.01825	0.9819	No causality
DBC does not Granger cause DUR		3.67790	0.0352**	Causality

Abbreviations: DCR: differenced credit risk; DBC: differenced bank capital; DEV: differenced earnings volatility; DNPL: differenced nonperforming loans; DBS: differenced bank size; INF: inflation; DUR: differenced unemployment rates
**5% level of significance
*10% level of significance

Table 4.17 Granger causality test for small banks (broad measure)

Null hypothesis	No. of observations	F-statistics	Probability	Conclusion
DCR does not Granger cause DLCBM	41	5.87706	0.0062**	Causality
DLCBM does not Granger cause DCR		0.20577	0.8150	No causality
Zscore does not Granger cause DLCBM	41	0.06831	0.9341	No causality
DLCBM does not Granger cause zscore		0.39151	0.6789	No causality
DEV does not Granger cause DLCBM	41	0.46040	0.6347	No causality
DLCBM does not Granger cause DEV		0.40235	0.6717	No causality
DNPL does not Granger cause DLCBM	41	3.22749	0.0514**	Causality
DLCBM does not Granger cause DNPL		1.29432	0.2865	No causality
DBS does not Granger cause DLCBM	41	1.93057	0.1598	No causality
DLCBM does not Granger cause DBS		0.13804	0.8715	No causality
DMS does not Granger cause DLCBM	41	7.65857	0.0017**	Causality
DLCBM does not Granger cause DMS		0.62184	0.5426	No causality
INF does not Granger cause DLCBM	41	0.49708	0.6124	No causality
DLCBM does not Granger cause INF		5.03281	0.0118**	Causality
DUR does not Granger cause DLCBM	41	2.40551	0.1046	No causality
DLCBM does not Granger cause DUR		0.13468	0.8744	No causality

Abbreviations: DCR: differenced credit risk; DLCBM: differenced liquidity creation broad measure; DEV: differenced earnings volatility; DNPL: differenced nonperforming loans; DBS: differenced bank size; INF: inflation; DUR: differenced unemployment rates
**5% level of significance
*10% level of significance

Table 4.18 Granger causality test for small banks (narrow measure)

Null hypothesis	No. of observations	F-statistics	Probability	Conclusion
DCR does not Granger cause DLCNM	41	0.42615	0.6563	No causality
DLCNM does not Granger cause DCR		1.66591	0.2033	No causality
Zscore does not Granger cause DLCNM	41	0.48310	0.6208	No causality
DLCNM does not Granger cause zscore		0.06859	0.9338	No causality
DEV does not Granger cause DLCNM	41	0.26749	0.7668	No causality
DLCNM does not Granger cause DEV		0.44217	0.6461	No causality
DNPL does not Granger cause DLCNM	41	2.11673	0.1352	No causality
DLCNM does not Granger cause DNPL		1.01557	0.3723	No causality
DBS does not Granger cause DLCNM	41	2.01560	0.1480	No causality
DLCNM does not Granger cause DBS		1.04391	0.3625	No causality
DMS does not Granger cause DLCNM	41	0.38397	0.6839	No causality
DLCNM does not Granger cause DMS		2.75944	0.0767*	Causality
INF does not Granger cause DLCNM	41	0.01494	0.9852	No causality
DLCNM does not Granger cause INF		0.44563	0.6439	No causality
DUR does not Granger cause DLCNM	41	0.71626	0.4954	No causality
DLCNM does not Granger cause DUR		1.39069	0.2620	No causality

Abbreviations: DCR: differenced credit risk; DLCNM: differenced liquidity creation narrow measure; DEV: differenced earnings volatility; DNPL: differenced nonperforming loans; DBS: differenced bank size; INF: inflation; DUR: differenced unemployment rates
**5% level of significance
*10% level of significance

Table 4.19 Granger causality test for small banks (capital)

Null hypothesis	No. of observations	F-statistics	Probability	Conclusion
DCR does not Granger cause DBC	41	2.75685	0.0769*	Causality
DBC does not Granger cause DCR		0.92405	0.4061	No causality
Zscore does not Granger cause DBC	41	0.02684	0.9735	No causality
DBC does not Granger cause zscore		2.74945	0.0774*	Causality
DEV does not Granger cause DBC	41	3.05798	0.0593*	Causality
DBC does not Granger cause DEV		2.47274	0.0986*	Causality
DNPL does not Granger cause DBC	41	1.17349	0.3208	No causality
DBC does not Granger cause DNPL		1.05019	0.3603	No causality
DBS does not Granger cause DBC	41	1.69688	0.1976	No causality
DBC does not Granger cause DBS		0.74679	0.4811	No causality
DMS does not Granger cause DBC	41	0.68783	0.5091	No causality
DBC does not Granger cause DMS		4.22178	0.0225**	Causality
INF does not Granger cause DBC	41	1.22919	0.3045	No causality
DBC does not Granger cause INF		0.24457	0.7843	No causality
DUR does not Granger cause DBC	41	0.46162	0.6339	No causality
DBC does not Granger cause DUR		0.11991	0.8874	No causality

Abbreviations: DCR: differenced credit risk; DBC: differenced bank capital; DEV: differenced earnings volatility; DNPL: differenced nonperforming loans; DBS: differenced bank size; INF: inflation; DUR: differenced unemployment rates
**5% level of significance
*10% level of significance

The time series dataset was constituted by individual banks' income statements as well as by BS and OBS items. In this regard, we differentiate between the broad (including BS and OBS items) and narrow measure (including BS items only) for liquidity creation. We choose the control variables, credit risk, z-score, earnings volatility, nonperforming loans, size, market share, inflation, and unemployment, for liquidity creation and capital (see, for instance, Subsection 4.4.1). All the variables were transformed into logarithms to avoid the problem of serial correlation and heteroskedasticity. Ultimately, before the data was analyzed, various steps were taken to ensure that the data was stationary. This was done because nonstationary variables may result in spurious regression that may indicate relationships between variables that do not exist.

Future research on liquidity creation and capital data will involve enhancing the approximation techniques for these variables. The process may be aided by the availability of more suitable data as well as improved extrapolation and interpolation techniques.

4.3.2 Implications (Granger Causality Test for Liquidity Creation and Capital Variables)

In the following, we highlight how our research on Granger causality for liquidity creation and bank capital has improved our understanding and advanced the knowledge in this field. From our main test (see Table 4.10) that involves bank capital and liquidity creation (broad and narrow measure) for large, medium, and small banks we can ascertain causality and directionality. In this context, changes to capital affects liquidity creation (narrow measure) and changes to liquidity creation (narrow measure) affects changes to capital for large and medium banks. In other words, the causality is bidirectional. Also, medium and small banks have a unidirectional causal relationship between capital and liquidity creation (*broad measure*). In addition, small banks experience similar associations between capital and liquidity creation (excluding OBS items).

In the sequel, we analyze some of our results in the light of existing literature on Granger causality for liquidity creation and bank capital. Our findings are similar to that of Horvath et al.[44] as well as Bouman and

Berger[45] regarding the vital role that capital plays in small banks. Large banks were found to be the primary contributors of liquidity creation in studies on Czech[46] and U.S. banks.[47] Having a more extensive dataset (38 countries), we found that this was true in both large and medium banks, but the causal relationship was bidirectional (Implication 4.3.9).

4.3.3 Implications (Granger Causality Tests for Liquidity Creation, Capital, and Control Variables for Large Banks)

We perform Granger causality tests involving liquidity creation, capital, and control variables for large banks as (see Question 4.1.3 in Subsection 4.1.3).

Given the obtained results, we develop new insights regarding the control variables that play a significant role in liquidity creation and capital for large banks. It is evident from Tables 4.11, 4.12, and 4.13 that the control variables that appear to have the most significant effect on large banks are earnings volatility, inflation, and bank size. Specifically, earnings volatility affects liquidity creation (broad measure) and capital. Also, inflation significantly affects liquidity creation and capital. Bank size plays an important bidirectional role in liquidity creation (narrow measure). However, capital affects bank size, in a unidirectional way.

4.3.4 Implications (Granger Causality Tests for Liquidity Creation, Capital, and Control Variables for Medium Banks)

We perform Granger causality tests involving liquidity creation, capital, and control variables for medium banks as referred to in Question 4.1.4 of Subsection 4.1.3.

Tables 4.14, to 4.16 show the results of causality tests that involve liquidity creation (broad and narrow measure) and capital with all the control variables for medium banks. It is apparent from the Granger causality model that several control variables significantly affect liquidity or capital, or both. For instance, credit risk affects liquidity creation (broad measure), z-score and nonperforming loans affect liquidity creation (narrow measure), and finally, inflation affects capital.

4.3.5 Implications (Granger Causality Tests for Liquidity Creation, Capital, and Control Variables for Small Banks)

We perform Granger causality tests involving liquidity creation, capital, and control variables for small banks as alluded to in Question 4.1.5 in Subsection 4.1.3. Tables 4.17 to 4.19 highlight that the control variables credit risk, nonperforming loans, and market share affect liquidity creation (broad measure or *including OBS items*). Credit risk and earnings volatility affect capital.

4.3.6 Implications (Basel III Policy Implications for Liquidity Creation and Capital)

Our findings have some policy implications for large, medium, and small banks. First, our results support the view that liquidity creation (*narrow measure*) might hamper banks' solvency, especially in large and medium banks. Second, capital can be used to predict liquidity creation for the narrow measure irrespective of bank size. Lastly, capital can be used in order to predict liquidity creation (*broad measure*) in medium and small banks. Similar to previous studies and extant theoretical literature, we agree that there is a trade-off between the benefits of financial stability induced by stronger capital requirements and those of greater liquidity creation. Therefore, favoring one objective might be detrimental to the other. This delicate balancing act is more critical in large and medium banks. Capital is the more prominent role player in small banks. Notably, these aforementioned relationships are further complicated by control variables that vary according to bank size.

In particular, three control variables (i.e., earnings volatility, inflation, and bank size) significantly affect liquidity creation and capital in large banks. Another three control variables (i.e., credit risk, z-score, and nonperforming loans) significantly impact liquidity creation, whereas inflation significantly affects capital in medium banks. However, five control variables impact liquidity creation and capital in small banks. More specifically, three control variables (i.e., credit risk, nonperforming loans, and market share) affect liquidity creation, and three control variables (i.e., credit risk, z-score, and earnings volatility) affect capital in small banks, respectively. This is indicative of how vulnerable small banks are to insolvency and bank failure.

Essentially, Basel III regulation should take the complicated relationship between bank capital, liquidity, and liquidity creation into account. However, this must not be done in isolation, but the aforementioned significant control variables, which differ according to bank size, should be considered.

4.4 How to Obtain the Results in Chapter 4

In this section, we discuss the methodology used to obtain the results presented in the previous section. The statistical package EViews 7 is used to perform our analyses.

4.4.1 How to Obtain Bank Liquidity Creation Results for Basel III

We compute two measures of liquidity creation and follow a similar approach as Berger and Bouman.[48] The classification is based on maturity of items as our data set provides detailed information that allows us to consider BS and OBS items by maturity. In other words, according to Berger and Bouwman[49] terminology, we consider the *mat fat* liquidity creation measure and the *mat nonfat* liquidity creation measure. For the purposes of our analysis, we label these measures as broad and narrow liquidity creation, respectively. The broad measure of liquidity creation incorporates OBS items that can also provide liquidity and are more comprehensive. On the other hand, the narrow measure is important as it enables us to check the robustness of our conclusions. Table 2.1 gives a detailed description of the liquidity classifications that we consider in this chapter.

The 11 variables involved in our study are briefly described as follows:[50]

1. Liquidity creation for the broad measure (including OBS items): the liquidity creation-to-assets ratio
2. Liquidity creation for the narrow measure (excluding OBS items): the liquidity creation-to-assets ratio

3. *Capital*: the bank equity-to-total assets ratio Control variables were added to account for the specific characteristics of the countries under analysis.

4. *Credit risk*: risk-weighted assets and OBS activities-to-assets ratio

5. *z-score*: return on assets plus capital-to-earnings volatility ratio

6. *Earnings volatility*: standard deviation of quarterly return on assets data

7. *Nonperforming loans*: nonperforming loans-to-total loans ratio

8. *Size*: log of total assets

9. *Market share*: share of total deposits

10. *Inflation*: year-on-year change in consumer prices

11. *Unemployment*: unemployment rate

Due to the different frequencies and measurements of the time series variables used in this study, we modify the variables for consistency and standardization purposes.[51] For instance, log transformation of variables is a very useful technique when using time series data. In other words, data was transformed into their natural logarithms to provide some uniformity and also to avoid some misspecification problems. In particular, to avoid problems of serial correlation and heteroskedasticity later, when conducting the Granger causality test.

4.4.2 How to Obtain a Granger Causality Framework for Basel III: Liquidity and Bank Capital

Another important theory that forms the basis of the methodology employed in the current chapter is that of Granger causality. This statistical hypothesis differentiates between *mere* correlations and identifies the presence or absence of causality and determines whether one time series is useful in forecasting another. In other words, Granger causality is a statistical concept of causality that is based on prediction. Its mathematical formulation is based on linear regression modeling of stochastic processes.[52]

In order to ascertain the causal link between bank capital and liquidity creation, we conduct a special test called the Granger causality test. In our study the standard Granger causality test amounts to testing whether past values of liquidity (LQDTY) together with past values of capital (CPTL) explains the current change in CPTL better than the past values of CPTL alone. Failure to reject this null hypothesis leads to the conclusion that LQDTY Granger causes CPTL. This process is repeated, interchanging the two variables (liquidity and capital). The Vector Autoregressive bivariate regressions of the form as follows will be esimated:

$$\text{CPTL}_t = \sum_{i=1}^{n} \alpha_{1i} \text{CPTL}_{t-1} + \sum_{j=1}^{n} \alpha_{2i} \text{LQDTY}_{t-j} + \mu_t \; \dots \qquad (4.1)$$

$$\text{LQDTY}_t = \sum_{i=1}^{n} \lambda_{1i} \text{LQDTY}_{t-1} + \sum_{j=1}^{n} \lambda_{2i} \text{CPTL}_{t-j} + \sigma_t \; \dots \qquad (4.2)$$

where CPTL_t stands for general bank CPTL and LQDTY_t for liquidity creation. μ_t and δ_t are the white noise terms. Using the general-to-specific approach, the lag length is chosen such that serial correlation is eliminated between the error terms. The following presents all possible causal relationships between two variables:

a) *Unidirectional causality* exists from LQDTY_t to CPTL_t if
$$\sum_{j=1}^{k} \alpha_{2j} \neq 0 \text{ and } \sum_{j=1}^{k} \lambda_{2j} = 0$$

b) *Unidirectional causality* exists from CPTL_t to LQDTY_t if
$$\sum_{i=1}^{k} \lambda_{2i} \neq 0 \text{ and } \sum_{j=1}^{k} \alpha_{2j} = 0$$

c) *Bidirectional causality* exists between CPTL_t and LQDTY_t if
$$\sum_{j=1}^{k} \lambda_{2j} \neq 0 \text{ and } \sum_{j=1}^{k} \alpha_{2j} \neq 0$$

d) *No causality* is established between CPTL_t and LQDTY_t if
$$\sum_{j=1}^{k} \alpha_{2j} = 0 \text{ and } \sum_{j=1}^{k} \lambda_{2j} = 0$$

The aforementioned formula was for CPTL and LQDTY. In addition to the main variables presented earlier, the Granger causality test will also be performed on all the other variables identified in this study.[53] Knowing the direction of causation will help the policy makers identify which variables to target first. Notably, theories generally do not distinguish between banks of different sizes. However, we do differentiate between different bank sizes because these distinctions are important from a policy perspective and for the empirical tests in this chapter.

CHAPTER 5

Basel III Liquidity Regulation and the Economy

In this chapter, for Class I and II banks, we identify liquidity risk sources as well as their management. Also, we discuss the connections between such risk and credit in the period before, during, and after the financial crisis.[1]

We note that Basel III liquidity regulation will increase intermediation costs that will, in turn, affect the global macroeconomy. In particular, we show that the implementation of Basel III will affect macroeconomic variables such as GDP, investment, inflation, consumption, personal disposable income (PDI), personal savings, and employment. In order to compensate for the higher funding cost, banks will increase lending spreads. To counteract this, return on equity and cost of bank debt must adjust accordingly.

In this chapter, we specifically quantify the envisaged intermediation costs for the South African economy in meeting Basel III's liquidity standards via appropriate adjustments. These costs depend on the implementation period, with longer periods leading to reduced output losses in exogenous scenarios. Furthermore, by comparison to the Macroeconomic Assessment Group (MAG) countries, the costs incurred are of similar size but marginally higher (H. Depp, personal communication, March–July 2013).

5.1 Background to Basel III Liquidity Regulation, the Crisis, and the Economy

In Section 5.2 of this chapter, we comment on credit extension that limits liquidity. This topic is highly relevant for appraising the economic impact of Basel III liquidity implementation.[2–4]

In Section 5.3, we examine the impact that the implementation of Basel III liquidity regulation will have on certain macroeconomic variables.[5-8] Here, Basel III intends to provide sufficient liquidity to allow ordered responses to liquidity restrictions. In this process, the new regulation imposes penalties for breaching the liquidity standards while allowing capital buffers to be built. It is costly to adjust balance sheets (BSs) and operating procedures to meet these standards. In this regard, banks and regulators alike are interested in the potential macroeconomic impact of Basel III's implementation. Implementation dates are also relevant as Basel III allows banks until 2015 to meet the short-term liquidity coverage ratio (LCR) and until 2018 for the longer term net stable funding ratio (NSFR).[9]

As a result of their elevated capital levels, banks in South Africa (SA) will not incur costly BS adjustments to meet Basel III capital requirements. However, substantial adjustment will be required to satisfy LCR and NSFR minimum standards. EMERG's dynamic stochastic general equilibrium (DSGE) quarterly model of the SA economy was used to estimate the potential cost of these adjustments.[10-14]

5.1.1 Review of Basel III Liquidity Regulation, the Crisis, and the Economy

In this subsection, we review Basel III liquidity regulation, the crisis, and their relationship with credit. A second thrust in our discussion is related to the impact of the implementation of Basel III on the South African macroeconomy.[15]

5.1.1.1 Review of Basel III Liquidity Regulation, the Crisis, and Credit

Gorton and Metrick show that, at the outset of the 2007 to 2009 financial crisis, in the U.S. repo market, mortgage-backed securities were largely financed by short-term borrowed funds.[16] However, by 08Q4, approximately 55% of each dollar invested in such securities could be financed this way. Unlike earlier recessions, loan balances continued to rise until almost 1 year into the crisis. This reflects movement of loans onto bank

BSs from preexisting off-balance sheet (OBS) commitments in the form of either credit lines or other guarantees.[17] For Class I and II banks, we verify the sources of liquidity risk associated with the 2007 to 2009 financial crisis that had to be addressed by Basel III liquidity regulation (see Subsection 5.2.1).

Cornett et al. demonstrate how liquid assets and credit provisioning vary across banks.[18] Their research tests how banks managed sudden increases in loan demand from OBS loan commitments during the crisis. In this regard, our chapter shows that Class I and II banks with higher levels of preexisting commitments increased their high-quality liquid assets (HQLA) holdings and simultaneously reduced new credit extension. Our primary conclusion is that loan commitment drawdowns displaced new credit extension during the crisis.[19]

According to Schmieder, in the management of liquidity risk, a bank can combine liquidity buffers and transparency to hedge small and large refinancing needs.[20] A bank that can assert its solvency will be able to attract external refinancing. Furthermore, Ojo suggests that Basel III makes allowances for Central Bank reserves that serve as a means whereby commercial banks manage their liquidity risk.[21] Our contribution relates to the aforementioned in that we show how Class I and II banks managed the liquidity shock of the 2007 to 2009 financial crisis prior to the implementation of Basel III regulation (see Subsection 5.2.2).

5.1.1.2 Review of Basel III Liquidity Regulation and the Macroeconomy

The initial attempts to forecast the impact of Basel III liquidity regulation have, mainly involved macroeconomic effects.[22–25] These reports by the MAG of the Financial Services Board (FSB) and Basel Committee on Banking Supervision (BCBS) (referred to as the MAG reports) discuss the economic impact of the new liquidity requirements when they were being phased in. The report BCBS175[26] by a BCBS working group that analyses the long-term economic impact (benefits and costs) of Basel III is referred to as the long-term economic impact (LEI) report. This report takes different capital adequacy ratio (CAR) levels into account and considers whether the capital rules are accompanied by additional requirements for liquidity. "Long-term" refers to the assumption that banks have completed the transition to the new regulations on capital and liquidity. In the LEI report, expected net benefit is measured as the difference between expected benefits as measured by the decrease in the annual probability of a crisis multiplied by the cumulative costs of a crisis and the expected costs of new requirements for capital and liquidity. Such benefits vary according to assumptions about whether the crisis has permanent effects on output.[27] Much of our analysis in this chapter is based on principles contained in the LEI report.[28]

Literature suggests that the costs in terms of lost output due to the changes in liquidity requirements are likely to be modest and less than those estimated by the banking sector itself.[29–32] Moreover, the LEI report concludes that there will be significant benefits from these changes due to the lower incidence of financial crises and that these benefits outweigh the costs.[33] Our results are consistent with that of the aforementioned studies in that we find that the impact of the implementation of the Basel III liquidity ratios on the SA macroeconomy was modest for most of the variables (H. Depp, personal communication, March–July 2013).

Moreover, Gambacorta[34] focuses on the long run effects of the implementation of Basel III liquidity regulation on interest rates, lending, GDP, and bank profitability. In particular, that paper establishes a framework to estimate the effects of higher bank liquidity requirements on output and bank profitability. To estimate the long-term cost effect of both higher bank capital and liquidity requirements, Gambacorta uses a Vector Error Correction Model (VECM) to estimate the long run relationships among variables for the United Kingdom.[35] The current chapter includes more macroeconomic parameters than were studied in Gambacorta[36] in that, besides GDP, we also assess the impact of the implementation of the Basel III liquidity standards on investment, inflation, consumption, personal income, personal savings, and employment (H. Depp, personal communication, March–July 2013).

5.1.2 Basel III Liquidity Regulation and Economic Data

We use EMERG global liquidity data that consists of observations for London Interbank Offered Rate (LIBOR)-based banks for the period

2002 to 2012.[37] The sample studied in Section 5.2 is exactly the same as the 391 bank cohort considered in Chapters 3 and 4. In addition, we discuss data on SA needed for the analysis in Section 5.3 in more detail.

5.1.3 Chapter 5: Main Contributions

The main questions about Basel III liquidity regulation, credit, and the macroeconomy are listed as follows. The answers to these questions constitute the main contributions in this chapter:

- **Question 5.1.1 (Basel III and liquidity risk sources).** *For Class I and II banks, what were the sources of liquidity risk associated with the 2007 to 2009 financial crisis that had to be addressed by Basel III liquidity regulation? (See Subsection 5.2.1).*

- **Question 5.1.2 (Basel III and liquidity risk management).** *How did Class I and II banks manage the liquidity shock of the 2007 to 2009 financial crisis prior to the implementation of Basel III regulation? For instance, how did Class I and II banks boost their holdings of HQLAs as prescribed by Basel III liquidity regulation as a buffer during and after the 2007 to 2009 crisis? (See Subsection 5.2.2).*

- **Question 5.1.3 (GDP impact assessment of Basel III liquidity ratios implementation).** *What will the impact of the implementation of the Basel III liquidity ratios on real GDP in SA be? (See Subsection 5.3.1.1).*

- **Question 5.1.4 (investment impact assessment of Basel III liquidity standard implementation).** *What will the impact on SA real investment of the implementation of the Basel III liquidity standards be? (See Subsection 5.3.1.2).*

- **Question 5.1.5 (inflation impact assessment of Basel III liquidity ratios implementation).** *What will the impact of the implementation of the Basel III liquidity standards on inflation in SA be? (See Subsection 5.3.1.3).*

- **Question 5.1.6 (consumption impact assessment of Basel III liquidity standard implementation).** *What will* *the impact on SA real consumption of the implementation of the Basel III liquidity ratios be? (See Subsection 5.3.1.4).*

- **Question 5.1.7 (personal income impact assessment of Basel III liquidity ratios implementation).** *What will the impact of the implementation of the Basel III liquidity ratios on real personal disposable income (RPDI) in SA be? (See Subsection 5.3.1.5).*

- **Question 5.1.8 (personal savings impact assessment of Basel III liquidity ratios implementation).** *What will the effect on SA personal savings rate of the implementation of the Basel III liquidity ratios be? (See Subsection 5.3.1.6).*

- **Question 5.1.9 (employment impact assessment of Basel III liquidity ratios implementation).** *What will the impact of the implementation of the Basel III liquidity ratios on SA employment be? (See Subsection 5.3.1.7).*

5.2 Liquidity Risk and Credit

In this section, for Class I and II banks, we provide results about liquidity risk sources and management and their connections with credit availability in the period before, during, and after the 2007 to 2009 financial crisis.[38]

5.2.1 Liquidity Risk Sources

In this subsection, we consider sources of liquidity risk such as loans, OBS commitments, and total credit for Class I and II banks (see Figures 5.1 and 5.2).

5.2.1.1 Total BS Loans, OBS Unused Commitments, and Total Credit for Class I and II Banks

Figures 5.1 and 5.2 show how liquidity risk sources such as total BS loans (BSL) and OBS unused commitments (OB) affected total credit (TCR) before, during, and after the crisis.

For Class I banks, OBS loan commitments increased at a constant rate from 1990 to 2007. Total bank credit, including both BS and OBS credit commitments, started to fall by 07Q2 with the decline accelerating

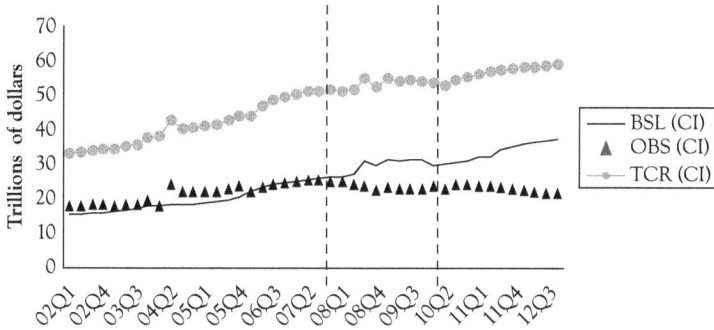

Figure 5.1 Total BS loans, OBS unused commitments, and total credit for Class I banks

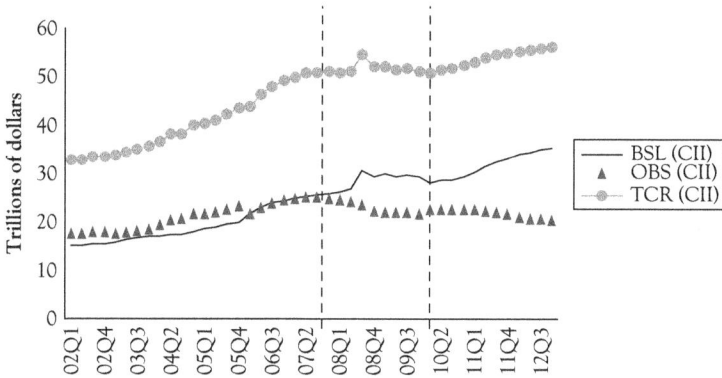

Figure 5.2 Total BS loans, OBS unused commitments, and total credit for Class II banks

sharply in 08Q4. By contrast, BS loans continued to rise until the end of 2008. The same trends as for Class I banks can be discerned for Class II banks except that from 04Q1 to 04Q3, there was a sharp rise and fall of OBS loan commitments for the latter.[39]

5.2.1.2 BS and OBS Credit Growth for Class I and II Banks

Figure 5.3 uses EMERG global banking data for 2002 to 2012 to illustrate BS and OBS credit growth.

Credit growth peaked for Class I banks in 04Q2, whereas such growth peaked for Class II banks in 08Q2. For the latter type of bank, this trend was followed by an extremely sharp decrease until 08Q4. All pronounced

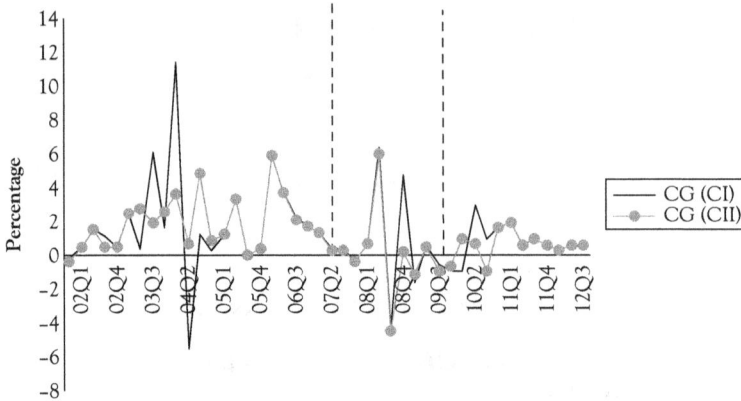

Figure 5.3 BS and OBS credit growth of Class I and II banks (2002–2012)

rises in credit growth were followed by sharp drops. Credit growth has been volatile in the period subsequent to the financial crisis. Furthermore, credit growth has been more volatile for Class I banks than their Class II counterparts throughout.

5.2.2 Liquidity Risk Management

The management of liquidity risk is a complex issue that usually involves BS and OBS adjustments. In order to make the discussion more palatable, we illustrate the main features of such management in the form of BS adjustments. This process is explained by using Table 5.1, where loan losses and provisions are ignored for ease of argument.

The upper tier of Table 5.1 illustrates how the BS of a hypothetical bank might have adjusted to liquidity pressures. It compares the bank's BS in 07Q1 to that of 09Q4. Before the crisis, the bank holds $425 billion in BS loans, with an additional $20 billion in OBS loan commitments and credit lines.[40] This results in total credit supply of $445 billion. The bank also holds $275 billion in HQLAs consisting of cash and other liquid assets. According to Petersen et al. 2013, on the liability side, the bank finances these assets with $300 billion from traditional deposits, $260 billion from wholesale short-term funding, and $60 billion from equity.[41]

Table 5.1 Illustration of adjustments to bank balance sheet ($ billions)

Assets		Liabilities	
Bank balance sheet before the crisis (in 07Q2)			
Cash (C)	50	Stable retail deposits (D^S)	150
Reserves (R)	25	Less stable retail deposits (D^L)	150
Treasuries (T)	50	Unsecured wholesale funding (F^U)	210
Government bonds (B^G)	100	100 interbank borrowings (B^I)	80
Corporate bonds (B^C)	50	Central bank borrowings (B^C)	50
Retail loans (Λ)	425	Equity (E)	60
Total	700	Total	700
OBS loan commitments			
Bank balance sheet after the crisis (end of 09Q4)			
Cash (C)	60	Stable retail deposits (D^S)	150
Reserves (R)	25	Less stable retail deposits (D^L)	150
Treasuries (T)	50	Unsecured wholesale funding (F^U)	280
Government bonds (B^G)	100	Interbank borrowings (B^I)	80
Corporate bonds (B^C)	50	Central bank borrowings (B^C)	50
Retail loans (Λ)	425	Equity (E)	60
Total	710	Total	710
OBS loan commitments			
Asset-side changes			
OBS loan commitments taken down			+10
Existing loans come due			−10
New loans by banks			0
HQLA increase			+10
Liability-side changes			
Interbank borrowings falls			−15
Deposits increase			+20
Central Bank borrowings			+5

The lower tier of Table 5.1 suggests that, during the 2007 to 2009 crisis, borrowers withdrew funds from existing commitments, lowering the OBS account from $20 to $10 billion and leaving BS loans unchanged at $425 billion. At the same time, the bank loses half its short-term funds as markets implode while nontraditional deposits, in the form of unsecured wholesale funding worth $20 billion, flow in. As a consequence, the bank is able to borrow an additional $5 billion from the central bank. Due to BS pressure from both the asset and liability sides, the bank strives to protect itself against disruptions by increasing its HQLAs from $275 to $285 billion via cash. Furthermore, the bank has no choice but to scale back its overall credit extension. In this illustration, new credit extension stops while total credit decreases from $445 billion to $435 billion upon the maturity of some loans

5.3 Basel III Liquidity Regulation and the Macroeconomy

Attempts to study the impact of Basel III liquidity regulation began with a consideration of macroeconomic effects.[42,43] Banking crises are typically triggered by pressures on their liquidity positions in the form of difficulties over financing their portfolios of assets.[44,45]

Given the MAG methodology[46-48] (see also Subsection 5.5.2), the impact of the implementation of Basel III liquidity regulation is reported for real GDP, real investment, CPI inflation, real consumption, RPDI, real savings rate, and employment. In each case, we display endogenous (denoted by "N") and exogenous (denoted by "X") scenarios for each of three adjustment paths.

5.3.1 Basel III Liquidity Regulation and Macroeconomic Variables

Table 5.2 summarizes the quarterly average reference processes of the aforementioned macroeconomic variables for the SA economy given EMERG's policy analysis or forecasting model and certain assumptions about global economic conditions (H. Depp, personal communication, March–July 2013).

In the ensuing subsections, we display the dynamics of the envisaged value of the macroeconomic variable under Basel III liquidity regulation— value of the average reference macroeconomic variable for each quarter in the period 13Q1 to 18Q4. Here, a positive value means that the envisaged value of the macroeconomic variable under Basel III liquidity regulation is higher than that of the average reference macroeconomic variable.

5.3.1.1 GDP

In Figure 5.4, we exhibit the dynamics of the Envisaged value of the real GDP under Basel III liquidity regulation—value of the average

Table 5.2 Annual average reference processes for the macroeconomic variables

Variables	2013	2014	2015	2016	2017	2018
Real GDP growth	2.30%	2.50%	2.60%	2.50%	2.80%	2.90%
Real GDP level*	2032.9	2113.7	2200.3	2288.4	2386.8	2479.8
Real investment*	480.7	506.1	532.7	557.9	581.6	605.6
Real consumption*	1364.5	1419.3	1474.2	1530.5	1559.7	1620.3
Prime interest rate	8.50%	8.50%	8.00%	8.00%	7.50%	7.50%
Inflation rate	6.00%	6.90%	6.30%	6.20%	6.10%	5.80%
Real wage growth	4.00%	3.90%	3.70%	3.70%	3.40%	3.40%
Employment**	8.43	8.61	8.81	9.00	9.15	9.32
RPDI growth	4.30%	4.30%	4.20%	4.20%	4.00%	3.90%
Personal saving PDI	0.20	0.40	0.76	1.17	1.22	1.26

* – In billion rands; ** – In million rands

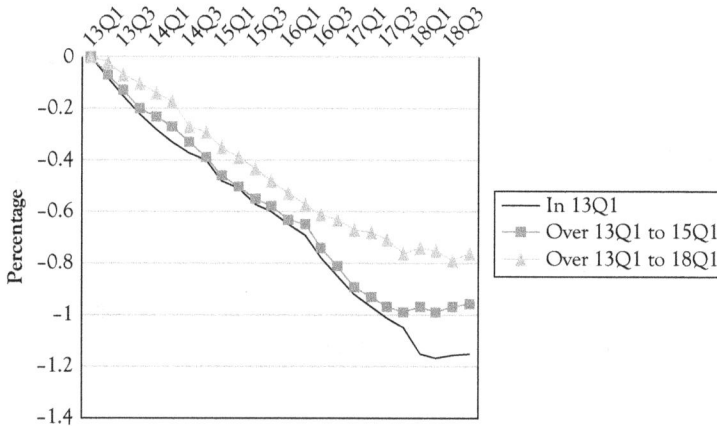

Figure 5.4 Difference between real GDP and the average reference level of real GDP (as percentage of reference GDP) for 13Q1, 13Q1–15Q1 and 13Q1–18Q1 Basel III liquidity regulation implementation

reference real GDP for each quarter in the period 13Q1 to 18Q4 if liquidity regulation comes into effect in 13Q1, in 2 years time and 5 years time.

While the graphs in Figure 5.4 traced the change in the level of GDP output from the reference GDP, Table 5.3 displays the value of the difference between the real GDP for the X and N policies under Basel III liquidity regulation and the average reference level of real GDP at the end

Table 5.3 Level impact of Basel III liquidity regulation on real GDP

Date/Period of Basel III liquidity regulation implementation	X policy		N policy	
	Largest change	End of 2018	Largest change	End of 2018
In 13Q1	–1.17%	–1.15%	–0.37%	–0.07%
Over 13Q1 to 15Q1	–0.99%	–0.96%	–0.22%	–0.11%
Over 13Q1 to 18Q1	–0.79%	–0.76%	–0.19%	–0.12%

of 2018 (percentage of reference real GDP in 18Q4) as well as its largest recorded change over the period 13Q1 to 18Q1.

5.3.1.2 Investment

In Figure 5.5, we map the Envisaged value of real investment under Basel III liquidity regulation—value of the average reference real investment for the period 13Q1 to 18Q4 if Basel liquidity regulation comes into effect in 13Q1, in 2 years time and 5 years time.

For the three implementation dates of Basel III liquidity regulation, Table 5.4 displays the value of the difference between real investment for the X and N policies and the average reference level of real investment at the end of 2018 (percentage of reference investment in 18Q4) as well as its largest recorded change over the period 13Q1 to 18Q4.

5.3.1.3 Inflation

In Figure 5.6, we exhibit the dynamics of the Envisaged value of CPI inflation under Basel III liquidity regulation—value of the average reference CPI inflation for each quarter in the period 13Q1 to 18Q4 if Basel liquidity regulation comes into effect in 13Q1, in 2 years time and 5 years time.

Table 5.5 displays the value of the difference between the CPI inflation for the X and N policies under Basel III liquidity regulation and the average reference level of CPI inflation at the end of 2018 (percentage of reference CPI inflation in 18Q4) as well as its largest recorded change over the period 13Q1 to 18Q1.

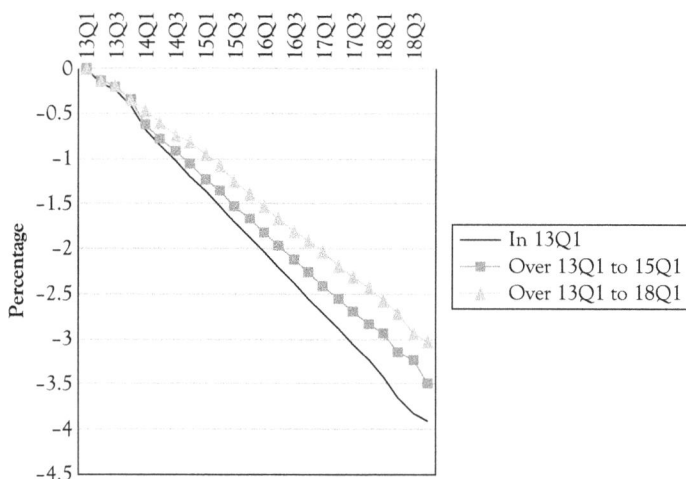

Figure 5.5 *Difference between real investment and the average reference level of real investment (as percentage of reference investment) for 13Q1, 13Q1–15Q1 and 13Q1–18Q1 Basel III liquidity regulation implementation*

Table 5.4 *Level impact of Basel III liquidity regulation on real investment*

Date/Period of Basel III liquidity regulation implementation	X policy		N policy	
	Largest change	End of 2018	Largest change	End of 2018
In 13Q1	–3.91%	–3.91%	–0.54%	–0.54%
Over 13Q1 to 15Q1	–3.49%	–3.49%	–0.52%	–0.52%
Over 13Q1 to 18Q1	–3.02%	–3.02%	–0.57%	–0.57%

5.3.1.4 Consumption

In Figure 5.7, we map the Envisaged value of real consumption under Basel III liquidity regulation - Value of the average reference real consumption for the period 13Q1 to 18Q4 if Basel III is implemented in 13Q1, in two years time and in 5 years time.

Table 5.6 displays the value of the difference between the real consumption for the X and N policies under Basel III liquidity regulation and the average reference level of real consumption at the end of 2018 (percentage of reference consumption in 18Q4) as well as its largest recorded change over the period 13Q1 to 18Q1.

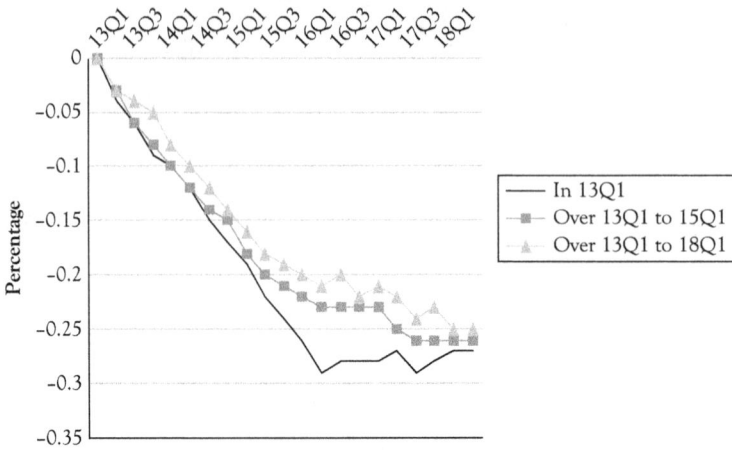

Figure 5.6 Difference between CPI inflation and the average reference level of CPI Inflation for 13Q1, 13Q1–15Q1 and 13Q1–18Q1 Basel III liquidity regulation implementation

Table 5.5 Level impact of Basel III liquidity regulation on CPI inflation

Date/Period of Basel III liquidity regulation implementation	X policy		N policy	
	Largest change	End of 2018	Largest change	End of 2018
In 13Q1	–0.29%	–0.27%	–0.08%	–0.07%
Over 13Q1 to 15Q1	–0.28%	–0.26%	–0.07%	–0.05%
Over 13Q1 to 18Q1	–0.25%	–0.25%	–0.05%	–0.04%

5.3.1.5 Personal Disposable Income

Figure 5.8 illustrates the differences between the baseline and Basel III scenarios for the level of RPDI.

Table 5.7 displays the value of the difference between the RPDI for the X and N policies under Basel III liquidity regulation and the average RPDI reference level at the end of 2018 (percentage of reference consumption in 18Q4) as well as its largest recorded change over the period 13Q1 to 18Q4.

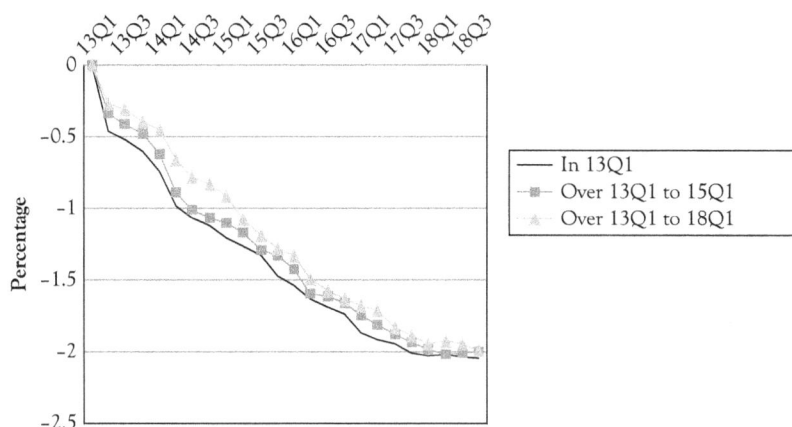

Figure 5.7 Difference between real consumption and the average reference level of real consumption (as percentage of reference consumption) for 13Q1, 13Q1–15Q1 and 13Q1–18Q1 Basel III liquidity regulation implementation

Table 5.6 Level impact of Basel III liquidity regulation on real consumption

Date/Period of Basel III liquidity regula- tion implementation	X policy		N policy	
	Largest change	End of 2018	Largest change	End of 2018
In 13Q1	−2.05%	−2.05%	−0.43%	−0.08%
Over 13Q1 to 15Q1	−2.02%	−2.00%	−0.28%	−0.23%
Over 13Q1 to 18Q1	−1.99%	−1.99%	−0.43%	−0.10%

5.3.1.6 Personal Savings Rate

In Figure 5.9, we display the dynamics of the Envisaged value of the personal savings rate under Basel III liquidity regulation—value of the average reference personal savings rate for each quarter in the period 13Q1 to 18Q4 when liquidity regulation comes into effect in 13Q1 as well as over 2 and 5 years.

Table 5.8 displays the value of the difference between the personal savings rate for the X and N policies under Basel III liquidity regulation and the average reference level of the personal savings rate at the end of 2018 (percentage of the reference personal savings rate in 18Q4) as well as its largest recorded change over the period 13Q1 to 18Q1.

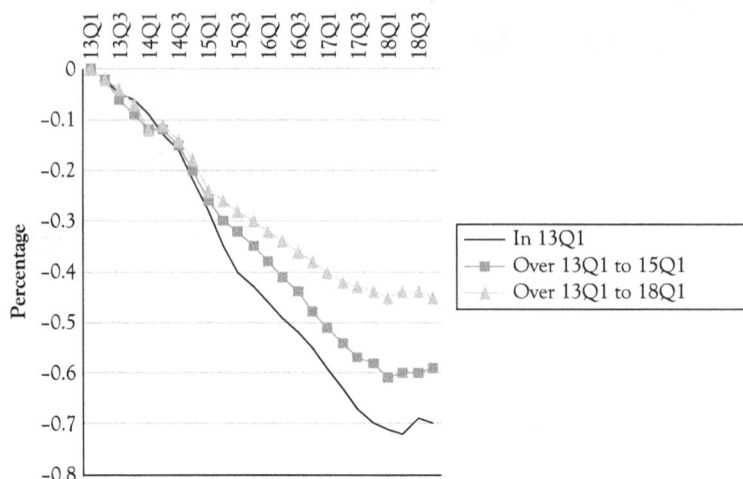

Figure 5.8 Difference between real consumption and the average reference level of real consumption (as percentage of reference consumption) for 13Q1, 13Q1–15Q1 and 13Q1–18Q1 Basel III liquidity regulation implementation

Table 5.7 Level impact of Basel III liquidity regulation on real personal disposable income (RPDI)

Date/Period of Basel III liquidity regulation implementation	X policy		N policy	
	Largest change	End of 2018	Largest change	End of 2018
In 13Q1	–0.72%	–0.70%	–0.61%	–0.04%
Over 13Q1 to 15Q1	–0.61%	–0.59%	–0.14%	–0.06%
Over 13Q1 to 18Q1	–0.45%	–0.45%	–0.12%	–0.08%

5.3.1.7 Employment

In Figure 5.10, we display the dynamics of the Envisaged value of employment under Basel III liquidity regulation—value of the average reference employment for each quarter in the period 13Q1 to 18Q4 when liquidity regulation comes into effect in 13Q1 as well as in 2 and 5 years time.

Table 5.9 displays the value of the difference between employment for the X and N policies under Basel III liquidity regulation and the average reference employment level at the end of 2018 (percentage of reference employment in 18Q4) as well as its largest recorded change over the period 13Q1 to 18Q1.

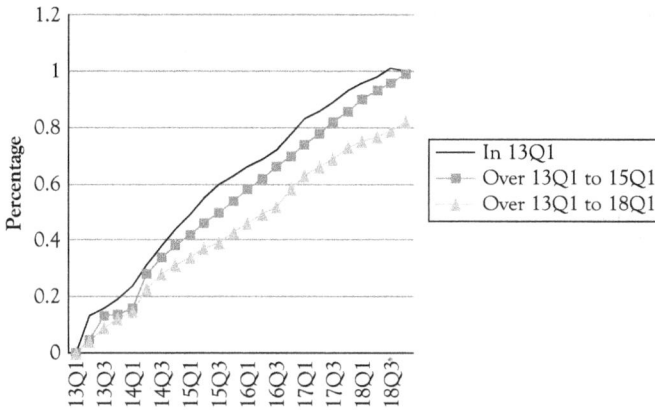

Figure 5.9 Difference between personal savings rate and the average reference personal savings rate for 13Q1, 13Q1–15Q1 and 13Q1–18Q1 Basel III liquidity regulation implementation

Table 5.8 Impact of Basel III liquidity regulation on personal savings rate by 18Q4

Date/Period of Basel III liquidity regulation implementation	X policy		N policy	
	Largest change	End of 2018	Largest change	End of 2018
In 13Q1	1.01%	1.00%	0.22%	0.02%
Over 13Q1 to 15Q1	0.99%	0.99%	0.19%	0.11%
Over 13Q1 to 18Q1	0.82%	0.82%	0.15%	0.06%

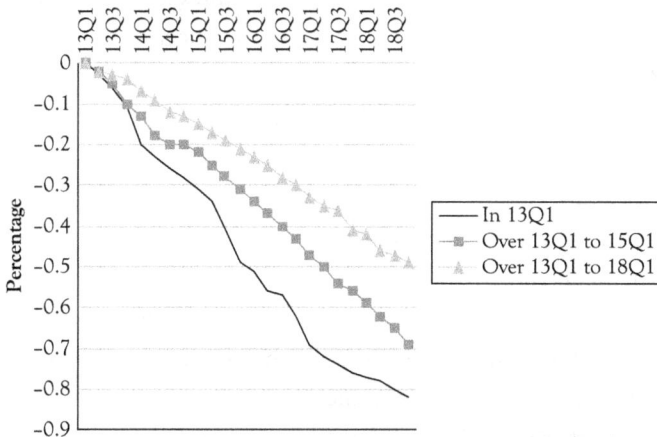

Figure 5.10 Difference between employment and the average reference level of employment (as percentage of reference employment) for 13Q1, 13Q1–15Q1 and 13Q1–18Q1 Basel III liquidity regulation implementation

Table 5.9 Impact of Basel III liquidity regulation on employment

Date/Period of Basel III liquidity regulation implementation	X policy		N policy	
	Largest change	End of 2018	Largest change	End of 2018
In 13Q1	–0.82%	–0.82%	–0.11%	–0.07%
Over 13Q1 to 15Q1	–0.69%	–0.69%	–0.11%	–0.08%
Over 13Q1 to 18Q1	–0.49%	–0.49%	–0.11%	–0.10%

5.4 Implications of Basel III Liquidity Regulation and the Economy

In this section, we draw conclusions about the results of Basel III liquidity regulation on the economy. For obvious reasons, liquidity risk sources and their management became important issues during and after the financial crisis. Our overall impression of the impact of Basel III liquidity regulation on the macroeconomy is that costly adjustments will be required to satisfy the LCR and NSFR.

5.4.1 Implications (Basel III and Liquidity Risk Sources)

The answer to Question 5.1.1 in Subsection 5.1.3 is that the main sources of liquidity risk for Class I and II banks associated with the 2007 to 2009 financial crisis were total BS loans and OBS unused commitments. One of the main objectives of Basel III regulation is to negate these risk sources. Such BS and OBS items affect total credit before, during, and after the crisis (see Subsection 5.2.1 for further discussion).

For Class I banks, the rise in BS loans during the crisis were due to borrowers drawing down preexisting credit lines. Banks began reducing loan extension by 07Q2. This illustrates how bank obligations to existing borrowers badly affected new borrowers. For nonbank brokerage firms, the collapse of the repo market proved disastrous. However, it was less of a problem for commercial Class I and II banks since deposit increases were used to overcome financing deficiencies.

We note that Class I and II banks finance their BS items with more than just deposits and equity. Other financing liabilities include repos, uninsured wholesale deposits and other short-term unsecured debt instruments. During the crisis, there was a scarcity of these sources of funds. For example, more often than not, repos were used to finance risky assets such as private-label securities. Gorton and Metrick[49] show that by 07Q2, such securities could be almost completely financed with short-term borrowed funds in the repo market.[50] However, by 08Q4, only 55% of each dollar invested in such securities could be financed this way. Banks that used repos to finance purchases of securities were confronted with a problem.[51,52] They faced big losses by selling securities in a collapsing market or they could access new and expensive credit.[53,54]

5.4.2 Implications (Basel III and Liquidity Risk Management)

Class I and II banks managed the liquidity shock of the 2007 to 2009 financial crisis by adjusting BS items (refer to Question 5.1.2). Table 5.1 shows how exposure to liquidity risk affected bank behavior in several respects. On the asset side, banks holding illiquid OBS securities increased cash buffers and decreased new credit extension during the crisis. Such banks were concerned about their ability to finance securitized assets and protected themselves by hoarding liquidity. Of course, this action badly affected borrowers. As far as the liability side is concerned, banks with a heavy reliance on wholesale sources of funding decreased new credit extension more drastically than banks that relied predominantly on traditional deposits and equity capital for funding (see Subsection 5.2.2 for more details).

The banks boosted their holdings of HQLAs as a buffer during and after the crisis while reducing new credit extension significantly (see, Question 5.1.3). As a result, loan commitment drawdowns displaced new credit extension during the 2007 to 2009 crisis. This situation highlights the importance of traditional deposits as a stabilizing source of funds and undrawn commitments as a potentially destabilizing source of asset side liquidity exposure.[55] The exercising of OBS commitments with their accompanying cash demands were a major reason why bank credit extension fell during the crisis (see Subsection 5.2.2 for further analysis).

Bank aggregate liquidity is determined by central banks so that focusing on liquidity risk management informs us about the activities of these banks.[56]By contrast, literature describes how cash, other HQLAs, and credit provision are different for various Class I and II banks.[57] During the 2007 to 2009 crisis, these variations helped explain differences in bank behavior.[58]

5.4.3 Implications (Impact on GDP of Basel III Liquidity Ratio Implementation)

From Figure 5.4 and Table 5.3 in Subsection 5.3.1.1, we conclude that the impact of the implementation of the Basel III liquidity ratios on SA real GDP will be moderate (compare with Question 5.1.3). In booms, banks more readily accept risks related to maturity mismatches and rely on readily available short-term funding to meet increasing loan demand. They might also have less interest in investing in banks as markets offer high yield investment opportunities for investors.

As elsewhere, in SA we expect that GDP growth will be negatively correlated with the LCR and NSFR. However, we have to be cautious in making such conclusions, since our results in Chapter 3 on Class I bank liquidity suggest that the opposite will happen for NSFRs (H. Depp, personal communication, March–July 2013).

Our results show that under exogenous monetary policy, a 75 bps adjustment in bank lending spreads would result in a maximum GDP loss of 1.17%, 0.99%, and 0.79% of baseline GDP for 13Q1, 8-quarter and 13Q1 to 18Q1 implementation. Implementation over 5 years resulted in a loss of between 0.12% and 0.8% of baseline GDP when both exogenous and endogenous scenarios are considered. These results are comparable with that of the MAG group that found that a 75 bps increase in spreads led to a median GDP loss of 0.6% of baseline (H. Depp, personal communication, March–July 2013).

Compliance with the Basel III regulatory proposals would, therefore, have cost implications for the output of the SA economy notwithstanding the anticipated benefits in terms of enhanced financial stability. The costs vary according to the period over which these regulatory changes are to be implemented, with longer implementation periods leading to smaller GDP losses in internationally comparable exogenous scenarios. Additionally, the incurred costs are marginally higher than those for the MAG countries but of similar size (H. Depp, personal communication, March–July 2013).

A discussion about the real GDP gap in Table 5.3 under the N scenario is given further on. When the interest rate and macroeconometric model is solved simultaneously, tighter interest rates lead not only to costs but also to a different environment for monetary policy. Higher spreads will, amongst other effects, imply more rapid disinflation as real wage increases are retarded by restrictive labor market conditions. This situation leads to a more lenient stance on monetary policy. For endogenous monetary policy, this economic adjustment is automatic. This explains why the cumulative GDP output cost is lower compared with the exogenous interest rate scenario.

The cost of Basel III implementation is affected by the length of the implementation period. At maximum deviation and 18Q4, under exogenous monetary policy, banks with longer implementation periods show smaller GDP losses relative to the baseline. By contrast, under endogenous interest rates, the response of monetary policy to elevated spreads inhibits maximum deviation and 18Q4 GDP losses when the implementation period is shorter (H. Depp, personal communication, March–July 2013).

A next step in our research on the impact on GDP of Basel III liquidity ratio implementation will involve analyzing improved Basel III liquidity ratio data. In this case, a more meaningful comparison between the effect on GDP of Class I and Class II banks may be possible. A wider range of test results may also be determined.

5.4.4 Implications (Investment Impact Assessment of Basel III Liquidity Ratio Implementation)

From Subsection 5.3.1.2, we conclude that the impact of the implementation of Basel III liquidity standards on SA investment is expected to be modest (compare with Question 5.1.4). However, under Basel III, investors are less likely to invest in bank debt or equity issuance because an accompanying reduction in dividends will enable banks to rebuild capital bases instead.

As far as investment is concerned, institutional profitability will probably decrease significantly under Basel III liquidity regulation. Also, an inherent feature of proposed Basel III regulation on nonequity instruments could start to make debt instruments loss absorbing prior to liquidation. This will negatively affect investment as a result of the elevated cost of new capital issuance and interbank lending rate (H. Depp, personal communication, March–July 2013).

Future research on investment impact assessment of Basel III liquidity ratio implementation will involve considering whether banks will change their funding profile that may lead to increased demand for longer term funding. Institutional investors may not be able or willing to provide funding as they avoid acquiring shares in the financial sector.

5.4.5 Implications (Impact on Inflation of Basel III Liquidity Standard Implementation)

Subsection 5.3.1.5 demonstrates that the overall impact of the implementation of the Basel III liquidity ratios on SA inflation will be modest (compare with Question 5.1.5).However, we anticipate that Basel III liquidity regulation will lead to SA banks experiencing notable inflation in their regulatory capital as a result of unrealized gains and losses.

We note that the implementation of LCR and NSFR standards together with increased capital requirements will increase the costs of starting foreign banks in SA. This will increase the cost of foreign trade credit that may lead to the depreciation of weaker currencies, costlier imports, and inflationary trends. Continued high inflation in SA as well as fiscal, trade, and current account deficits has led to growth retardation, which could further impact liquidity (H. Depp, personal communication, March–July 2013).

Future research on the impact of Basel III liquidity standard implementation on inflation should consider the impact of HQLAs on inflation risk and its enhancement of liquidity. Also, an investigation into relationships between liquidity, price stability, and levels of inflation should be interesting.

5.4.6 Implications (Impact on Consumption of Basel III Liquidity Standard Implementation)

Subsection 5.3.1.6 demonstrates that the overall impact of the implementation of the Basel III liquidity ratios on SA consumption will be modest (compare with Question 5.1.6).

In the exogenous monetary policy scenario, for consumption, the longer the implementation period, the lower the maximum as well as the 18Q4 deviation. The same is true for the endogenous scenario with the exception of the deviation at the end of 2018. The phasing in of Basel III liquidity regulation over 8 quarters has a greater effect than both 13Q1 and 13Q1 to 18Q1 implementation. In SA, these trends may be more to do with factors such as culture, income, weather, economic structure, and degree of urbanization than Basel III (H. Depp, personal communication, March–July 2013).

5.4.7 Implications (Impact on Personal Income of Basel III Liquidity Ratio Implementation)

From Subsection 5.3.1.7, we conclude that the impact of the implementation of the Basel III liquidity ratios on SA personal income will be modest depending, for instance, on legislation on revenue.

For bank shareholders, the pro-rata share of earnings must be reported on personal income returns that create a tax obligation. This expense is negated when the bank pays dividends to shareholders. However, if Basel III liquidity regulation is adopted, the bank could, under certain circumstances, be restricted or prohibited from paying dividends. However, the shareholder is still obligated to pay the same taxes regardless of whether the bank pays dividends or not. As a result, the implementation of Basel III regulation will negatively impact personal income (H. Depp, personal communication, March–July 2013).

5.4.8 Implications (Personal Savings Impact Assessment of Basel III Liquidity Ratio Implementation)

The impact of the implementation of the Basel III liquidity ratios on SA personal savings rate will be modest (compare with Question 5.1.7).

At present, theoretical macroeconometric models are undecided about the impact of higher interest rates on personal savings. This is due to the fact that substitution and income effects have opposite impacts. Furthermore, there are reasons why savings might not be impacted by interest rates in developing economies like South Africa. Results suggest a modest positive response of savings to an increase in real interest rates. However, this response must be understood in context. In the EMERG model, savings is calculated as the residual of household consumption. As a result, the decision by consumers to save is not conscious, but rather savings is calculated as the difference between disposable income and consumption spending. Consequently, an increase in interest rates leading to a positive response in savings may result from a decrease in interest sensitive consumption rather than a discretionary increase in household savings.

In SA, low personal savings levels are increasing the difficulties encountered by banks in satisfying certain Basel III requirements. In fact, because of low interest rates offered, banks themselves may make it difficult for South Africans to save. By 2013, deposits by SA firms and financial institutions accounted for 61.2% of total deposits, retail or household deposits made up 25.4%, nonresidents contributed 3.6%, and the balance came from other deposit types. This structure of deposits and, hence, personal savings, presents a challenge for SA banks in meeting Basel III requirements (H. Depp, personal communication, March–July 2013).

Under Basel III liquidity regulation, a number of different classes, or funding sources, may be identified. Thus far, banks have credit unions as stable depositors, with favorable rates of return offered to them. In the event of Basel III implementation, it appears that deposits from credit unions will be classified as unsecured wholesale funding rather than retail or small business deposits. In a stress scenario, deposits from unsecured sources would in all likelihood be withdrawn from banks. Consequently, such deposits especially those with maturities of less than one year, would become an unstable source of funding and loose its appeal for banks. In this case, the interest rates offered to credit unions may decrease and the impact on personal savings will be felt in unions that offer personal savings packages.

Future research will involve improving on the personal savings model in several respects. We believe that improved models will make the prediction of the impact on personal savings of Basel III liquidity ratio implementation more reliable. Also, with an enhanced model, the secondary effects of Basel III on personal savings may be studied more comprehensively.

5.4.9 Implications (Impact on Employment of Basel III Liquidity Standard Implementation)

From Subsection 5.3.1.9, we have that the increase in lending spreads occurs endogenously as one response to the aforementioned regulation.

Due to imperfect substitutability between market financing and bank credit, this leads to lower investment, which then affects employment and output. In the short run, the reduction in aggregate demand should reduce inflationary pressures. This should induce a monetary policy easing, which could partially offset the increase in lending spreads.

5.5 How to Obtain the Results in Chapter 5

In this section, we show how the main results in Chapter 5 about the effect of the implementation of Basel III liquidity standards on the SA macroeconomy are obtained. In particular, we show how to choose a macroeconometric model for SA. Next, we highlight the salient features of the MAG methodology.

5.5.1 How to Use a Model for the SA Macroeconomy

For the estimation of the economic impact of the implementation of Basel III liquidity regulation in the LEI and MAG reports,[59-62] the new requirements were first translated into higher costs of intermediation (higher lending spreads). Subsequently, the impact of these intermediation costs on the economy were estimated through macroeconometric models. In this regard, banks are likely to raise the cost of loan extension, lower the volume of lending, or some combination of these to make the necessary adjustments needed for Basel III liquidity requirements.

In order to do the study the required adjustments for the SA economy, EMERG's quarterly DSGE model of the SA economy was used to estimate the potential costs.[63] This model enables us to follow the methodology employed by the MAG in investigating the macroeconomic implications of Basel III liquidity regulation (see Subsection 5.5.3 for more details). However, the capacity of markets to accommodate these adjustments is not easily addressed by macroeconometric models. This is especially true as all international and SA banks will be changing their BS structures simultaneously.

In the SA context, we would like to adopt a methodology and assumptions similar to that of the MAG. Their methodology assumes that the implementation of Basel III liquidity requirements occurs without disruption and markets adapt seamlessly.[64-66] The idiosyncrasies of the SA market adaptation will require model monitoring and feedback that allow for structural changes to banks and credit availability. In our model, credit extension is driven by cost, where higher costs reduce credit demand and vice versa. Consequently, a SA economic impact assessment requires a model that provides an estimate of this increase in the cost of credit under appropriate conditions.[67–69]

5.5.2 How to Implement the MAG Methodology for the SA Macroeconomy

The contents of this subsection about the implementation of the MAG methodology for the SA macroeconomy was communicated personally (H. Depp, personal communication, March–July 2013).[70–72]

The MAG's satellite model subgroup was tasked with developing and implementing models that transmit Basel III capital and liquidity requirements into appropriate proxy parameters such as interest rate spreads and credit volumes.[73–75] These variables then served as inputs into policy analysis or forecasting models (such as the EMERG model) that measure the potential macroeconomic impact of Basel III regulatory changes in terms of reference levels of chosen macroeconomic variables.[76–78] A brief description of the two-step MAG methodology follows.

5.5.2.1 Step 1 in the MAG Methodology

The MAG collated the results of several sovereign-specific studies by group members.[79–81] These studies were conducted under various restrictions and reference conditions. However, in the policy analysis or forecasting modelling methodology used by most, the adjustment to Basel III was translated into a forecasted adjustment to interest rate spreads or credit volumes.[82–84]

5.5.2.2 Step 2 in the MAG Methodology

The second step of the MAG methodology considers Basel III interest rate spreads or credit volumes. In this step, we compute the outputs for the most important macroeconomic variables when compared with the reference levels of these variables.

Notes

Preface

1. Larson (2011, April).
2. Hong, Huang, and Wu (2013).
3. Berger and Bouwman (2009).
4. Macroeconomic Assessment Group (2011, October).

Chapter 1

1. Larson (2011, April).
2. Basel Committee on Banking Supervision(1988, July).
3. Basel Committee on Banking Supervision (2006, June).
4. Basel Committee on Banking Supervision (2004, June).
5. Basel Committee on Banking Supervision (2010a, December).
6. Basel Committee on Banking Supervision (2010b, December).
7. Larson (2011, April).
8. Larson (2011, April).
9. Larson (2011, April).
10. Basel Committee on Banking Supervision (1988, July).
11. Larson (2011, April).
12. Larson (2011, April).
13. Larson (2011, April).
14. Basel Committee on Banking Supervision (1988, July).
15. Larson (2011, April).
16. Basel Committee on Banking Supervision (1988, July).
17. Larson (2011, April).
18. Larson (2011, April).
19. Basel Committee on Banking Supervision (1988, July).
20. Basel Committee on Banking Supervision (1988, July).
21. Larson (2011, April).
22. Larson (2011, April)
23. Larson (2011, April).
24. Basel Committee on Banking Supervision (1988, July).
25. Basel Committee on Banking Supervision(2006, June).
26. Basel Committee on Banking Supervision(2004, June).
27. Basel Committee on Banking Supervision(2006, June).

28. Basel Committee on Banking Supervision(2004, June).
29. Basel Committee on Banking Supervision(2006, June).
30. Basel Committee on Banking Supervision(2004, June).
31. Basel Committee on Banking Supervision(2006, June).
32. Basel Committee on Banking Supervision(2004, June).
33. Basel Committee on Banking Supervision(2006, June).
34. Basel Committee on Banking Supervision(2004, June).
35. Larson (2011, April).
36. Basel Committee on Banking Supervision(2006, June).
37. Basel Committee on Banking Supervision(2004, June).
38. Larson (2011, April).
39. Basel Committee on Banking Supervision(2006, June).
40. Basel Committee on Banking Supervision(2004, June).
41. Larson (2011, April).
42. Basel Committee on Banking Supervision(2006, June).
43. Basel Committee on Banking Supervision(2004, June).
44. Basel Committee on Banking Supervision(2006, June).
45. Basel Committee on Banking Supervision(2004, June).
46. Larson (2011, April).
47. Larson (2011, April).
48. Larson (2011, April).
49. Basel Committee on Banking Supervision (2010a, December).
50. Basel Committee on Banking Supervision (2010b, December).
51. Basel Committee on Banking Supervision (2010a, December).
52. Basel Committee on Banking Supervision (2010b, December).
53. Basel Committee on Banking Supervision (2010a, December).
54. Basel Committee on Banking Supervision (2010b, December).
55. Larson (2011, April).
56. Basel Committee on Banking Supervision (2010a, December).
57. Basel Committee on Banking Supervision (2010b, December).
58. Larson (2011, April).
59. Larson (2011, April).
60. Larson (2011, April).
61. Basel Committee on Banking Supervision (2010a, December).
62. Basel Committee on Banking Supervision (2010b, December).
63. Moody's Analytic (2012).
64. Basel Committee on Banking Supervision (2010a, December).
65. Basel Committee on Banking Supervision (2010b, December).
66. Moody's Analytic (2012).
67. Moody's Analytic (2012).
68. Basel Committee on Banking Supervision (2010a, December).

69. Basel Committee on Banking Supervision (2010b, December).
70. Moody's Analytic (2012).
71. Basel Committee on Banking Supervision (2010a, December).
72. Basel Committee on Banking Supervision (2010b, December).
73. Moody's Analytic (2012).
74. Larson (2011, April).
75. Larson (2011, April).
76. Basel Committee on Banking Supervision (2010a, December).
77. Basel Committee on Banking Supervision (2010b, December).
78. Basel Committee on Banking Supervision (1988, July).
79. Basel Committee on Banking Supervision (2006, June).
80. Basel Committee on Banking Supervision(2004, June).
81. Basel Committee on Banking Supervision (2010, September).
82. Basel Committee on Banking Supervision (2010b, December).

Chapter 2

1. Basel Committee on Banking Supervision (2011, July).
2. Basel Committee on Banking Supervision (2008, September).
3. Petersen, De Waal, Mukuddem-Petersen, and Mulaudzi (2012a).
4. Petersen, Senosi, and Mukuddem-Petersen (2012b).
5. Bank for International Settlements (2011, February).
6. Basel Committee on Banking Supervision (2010a, December).
7. Schmieder, Hesse, Neudorfer, Puhr, and Schmitz (2012).
8. Petersen, De Waal, Mukuddem-Petersen, and Mulaudzi (2012a).
9. Berger, and Bouwman (2009).
10. Horvath, Seidler, and Weill (2012).
11. Basel Committee on Banking Supervision (2008, September).
12. Basel Committee on Banking Supervision (2013, January).
13. Basel Committee on Banking Supervision (2013, January).
14. Basel Committee on Banking Supervision (2010a, December).
15. Basel Committee on Banking Supervision (2009, December).
16. Petersen, Hlatshwayo, Mukuddem-Petersen, and Gideon (2013b).
17. Basel Committee on Banking Supervision (2013, January).
18. Basel Committee on Banking Supervision (2011, June).
19. Basel Committee on Banking Supervision (2010b, December).
20. Petersen, Hlatshwayo, Mukuddem-Petersen, and Gideon (2013b).
21. Petersen, De Waal, Mukuddem-Petersen, and Mulaudzi (2012a).
22. Basel Committee on Banking Supervision (2013, January).
23. Petersen, De Waal, Hlatshwayo, and Mukuddem-Petersen (2013a).
24. Basel Committee on Banking Supervision (2013, January).

25. Basel Committee on Banking Supervision (2013, January).
26. Petersen, Hlatshwayo, Mukuddem-Petersen, and Gideon (2013b).
27. Petersen, Senosi, and Mukuddem-Petersen (2012b).
28. Basel Committee on Banking Supervision (2013, January).
29. Petersen, De Waal, Mukuddem-Petersen, and Mulaudzi (2012a).
30. Petersen, De Waal, Mukuddem-Petersen, and Mulaudzi (2012a).
31. Petersen, Senosi, and Mukuddem-Petersen (2012b).
32. Petersen, De Waal, Mukuddem-Petersen, and Mulaudzi (2012a).
33. Basel Committee on Banking Supervision (2011, June).
34. Basel Committee on Banking Supervision (2010b, December).
35. Petersen, Senosi, and Mukuddem-Petersen (2012b).
36. Basel Committee on Banking Supervision (2011, June).
37. Basel Committee on Banking Supervision (2010b, December).
38. Petersen, De Waal, Mukuddem-Petersen, and Mulaudzi (2012a).
39. Cullen (2011).
40. Thornton (2009, May).
41. Basel Committee on Banking Supervision (2011, June).
42. Basel Committee on Banking Supervision (2010b, December).
43. Cullen (2011).
44. Berger and Bouwman (2009).
45. Diamond and Rajan (2001).
46. Diamond and Rajan (2000).
47. Allen and Gale (2004).
48. Allen and Santomero (2001).
49. Bhattacharya and Thakor (1993).
50. Repullo (2004).
51. Bhattacharya and Thakor (1993).
52. Repullo (2004).
53. Cornett, McNutt, Strahan, andTehranian (2011).
54. Petersen, Hlatshwayo, Mukuddem-Petersen, and Gideon (2013b).
55. Petersen, Senosi, and Mukuddem-Petersen (2012b).
56. Petersen, De Waal, Mukuddem-Petersen, and Mulaudzi (2012a).
57. Petersen, De Waal, Mukuddem-Petersen, and Mulaudzi (2012a).

Chapter 3

1. Wu and Hong (2012a); Wu and Hong (2012b); Hong, Huang, and Wu (2013).
2. Wu and Hong (2012a); Wu and Hong (2012b); Hong, Huang, and Wu (2013).
3. Petersen, Senosi, and Mukuddem-Petersen (2012b).
4. Basel Committee on Banking Supervision (2013, January).
5. Basel Committee on Banking Supervision (2013, January).

6. Petersen, De Waal, Mukuddem-Petersen, and Mulaudzi (2012a)
7. Gu (2011).
8. Basel Committee on Banking Supervision (2013, September).
9. Basel Committee on Banking Supervision (2013, March).
10. Basel Committee on Banking Supervision (2012, September).
11. Basel Committee on Banking Supervision (2012, April).
12. Basel Committee on Banking Supervision (2010, December).
13. European Banking Authority (2013, September).
14. European Banking Authority (2013, April).
15. European Banking Authority (2012, September).
16. European Banking Authority (2012, April).
17. Allen, Chan, Milne, and Thomas, (2010).
18. Wu and Hong (2012).
19. Basel Committee on Banking Supervision, (2013, September).
20. Gu (2011).
21. Distinguin, Roulet, and Tarazia. (2013).
22. Garleanu and Pedersen (2007).
23. Acharya, Gale, andYorulmazer, (2011).
24. Brunnermeier (2009).
25. Diamond and Rajan (2005).
26. He and Xiong (2012).
27. Wu and Hong (2012).
28. Wu and Hong (2012).
29. Hong, Huang, and Wu (2013).
30. Kullback (1959).
31. Wu and Hong (2012).
32. Wu and Hong (2012).
33. Hong, Huang, and Wu (2013).
34. Wu and Hong (2012).
35. Wu and Hong (2012).
36. Hong, Huang, and Wu (2013).
37. Wu and Hong (2012).
38. Wu and Hong (2012).
39. Hong, Huang, and Wu (2013).
40. Petersen, Hlatshwayo, Mukuddem-Petersen, and Gideon (2013b).
41. Petersen, De Waal, Hlatshwayo, and Mukuddem-Petersen (2013a).
42. Wu and Hong (2012).
43. Hong, Huang, and Wu (2013).
44. Wu and Hong (2012).
45. Hong, Huang, and Wu (2013).
46. EMERG (2013).

47. Basel Committee on Banking Supervision (2013, January).

48. EMERG (2013).

49. Basel Committee on Banking Supervision (2013, January).

50. Basel Committee on Banking Supervision (2013, January).

51. Basel Committee on Banking Supervision (2013, January).

52. Basel Committee on Banking Supervision (2013, January).

53. Basel Committee on Banking Supervision (2013, September).

54. Basel Committee on Banking Supervision (2013, March)

55. Basel Committee on Banking Supervision (2012, September).

56. Basel Committee on Banking Supervision (2012, April).

57. Basel Committee on Banking Supervision (2010, December).

58. European Banking Authority (2013, September).

59. European Banking Authority (2013, April).

60. European Banking Authority (2012, September).

61. European Banking Authority (2012, April).

62. Basel Committee on Banking Supervision (2013, September).

63. Basel Committee on Banking Supervision (2013, March).

64. Basel Committee on Banking Supervision (2012, September).

65. European Banking Authority (2013, September).

66. European Banking Authority (2013, April).

67. Basel Committee on Banking Supervision (2013, September).

68. Basel Committee on Banking Supervision (2013, March).

69. European Banking Authority (2013, September).

70. European Banking Authority (2013, April).

71. Wu and Hong (2012).

72. Hong, Huang, and Wu (2013).

73. Hong, Huang, and Wu (2013).

74. Kullback (1959).

75. Kullback (1959).

76. Wu and Hong (2012).

77. Hong, Huang, and Wu (2013).

78. Wu and Hong (2012).

79. Hong, Huang, and Wu (2013).

80. Wu and Hong (2012

81. Hong, Huang, and Wu (2013).

82. Wu and Hong (2012).

83. Wu and Hong (2012

84. Hong, Huang, and Wu (2013).

85. Wu and Hong (2012).

86. Hong, Huang, and Wu (2013).

87. Wu and Hong (2012).

88. Hong, Huang, and Wu (2013).

89. Wu and Hong (2012).

90. Hong, Huang, and Wu (2013).

91. Wu and Hong (2012).

92. Wu and Hong (2012).

93. Hong, Huang, and Wu (2013).

94. Wu and Hong (2012).

95. Hong, Huang, and Wu (2013).

96. Wu and Hong (2012).

97. Hong, Huang, and Wu (2013).

98. Wu and Hong (2012).

99. Hong, Huang, and Wu (2013).

100. EMERG (2013).

101. Wu and Hong (2012).

102. Hong, Huang, and Wu (2013).

103. Basel Committee on Banking Supervision (2013, January).

104. Wu and Hong (2012).

105. Hong, Huang, and Wu (2013).

106. Institute of International Finance (IIF) (June 2010).

107. EMERG (2013).

108. Basel Committee on Banking Supervision (2013, September).

109. Basel Committee on Banking Supervision (2013, March).

110. Basel Committee on Banking Supervision (2012, September).

111. Basel Committee on Banking Supervision (2012, April).

112. Basel Committee on Banking Supervision (2010, December).

113. European Banking Authority (2013, September).

114. European Banking Authority (2013, April).

115. European Banking Authority (2012, September).

116. European Banking Authority (2012, April).

117. Wu and Hong (2012a); Wu and Hong (2012b); Hong, Huang, and Wu (2013).

118. Kullback (1959).

119. Thomas, Edelman, and Crook (2002).

120. Kullback (1959).

121. Wu and Hong (2012).

122. Allen, Carletti, and Gale (2009).

123. Wu and Hong (2012).

124. Wu and Hong (2012).

125. Hong, Huang, and Wu (2013).

126. Wu and Hong (2012a); Wu and Hong (2012b); Hong, Huang, and Wu (2013).

127. Wu and Hong (2012a); Wu and Hong (2012b); Hong, Huang, and Wu (2013).

128. Thomas, Edelman, and Crook (2002).

129. Wu and Hong (2012a); Wu and Hong (2012b); Hong, Huang, and Wu (2013).
130. Wu and Hong (2012).
131. Wu and Hong (2012).
132. Wu and Hong (2012).
133. Wu and Hong (2012).
134. Wu and Hong (2012).
135. Wu and Hong (2012).
136. Wu and Hong (2012).
137. Wu and Hong (2012a); Wu and Hong (2012b); Hong, Huang, and Wu (2013).
138. Wu and Hong (2012a); Wu and Hong (2012b); Hong, Huang, and Wu (2013).
139. Wu and Hong (2012a); Wu and Hong (2012b); Hong, Huang, and Wu (2013).
140. Wu and Hong (2012a); Wu and Hong (2012b); Hong, Huang, and Wu (2013).
141. Wu and Hong (2012).

Chapter 4

1. Berger and Bouwman (2009).
2. Berger and Bouwman (2009).
3. Berger, Bouwman, Kick, and Schaek (2012).
4. Horvath, Seidler, and Weill (2012).
5. Liquidity creation: refers to the fact that banks give illiquid loans to borrowers while providing depositors the ability to withdraw funds at par value at a moment's notice. Diamond and Rajan (2001).
6. Small banks with gross total assets (GTA) up to $1 billion, medium banks with GTA $1 billion—$3 billlion and large banks with GTA exceeding 3 billion (measured in real 2003 dollars).
7. Berger and Bouwman (2009).
8. Berger, Bouwman, Kick, and Schaek (2012).
9. Berger, Bouwman, Kick, and Schaek (2012).
10. Bernanke (1983).
11. Acharya, Gale, and Yorulmazer, (2011).
12. Horvath, Seidler, and Weill (2012).
13. Horvath, Seidler, and Weill (2012).
14. Horvath, Seidler, and Weill (2012).
15. Horvath, Seidler, and Weill (2012).
16. Berger and Bouwman (2009).
17. Distinguin, Roulet, and Tarazia (2013).
18. Distinguin, Roulet, and Tarazia (2013).
19. Berger and Bouwman (2009).
20. Berger and Bouwman (2009).
21. Berger, Bouwman, Kick, and Schaek (2012).
22. Horvath, Seidler, and Weill (2012).

23. Distinguin, Roulet, and Tarazia (2013).
24. Berger and Bouwman (2009).
25. Diamond and Rajan (2000).
26. Diamond and Rajan (2001).
27. Allen and Santomero (2001).
28. Allen and Gale (2004).
29. Bhattacharya and Thakor (1993).
30. Repullo (2004).
31. Bhattacharya and Thakor (1993).
32. Repullo (2004).
33. Berger and Bouwman (2009).
34. EMERG (2013).
35. Berger and Bouwman (2009).
36. Berger, Bouwman, Kick, and Schaek (2012).
37. Horvath, Seidler, and Weill (2012).
38. Distinguin, Roulet, and Tarazia (2013).
39. Small, medium, and large banks were measured in real 2003 dollars.
40. Leptokurtosis is a common feature in economic or financial data that shows that the series tend to have an excessive peak at the mean and rather fat tails in the distribution.
41. Regarding *Jarque-Bera, the* H_o of a normal distribution is rejected if the *p*-value < 5%.
42. It is a method of deciding whether to reject a null hypothesis, and it involves comparing a sample statistic with critical values; see Studenmund, A. H. (2011). *Using econometrics: A practical guide*, Boston, Pearson Education.
43. Granger (1969).
44. Horvath, Seidler, and Weill (2012).
45. Bouwman and Berger (2009).
46. Horvath, Seidler, and Weill (2012).
47. Berger and Bouwman (2009).
48. Berger and Bouwman (2009).
49. Berger and Bouwman (2009).
50. Horvath, Seidler, and Weill (2012).
51. Horvath, Seidler, and Weill (2012).
52. Granger (1969).
53. Granger (1969).

Chapter 5

1. Cornett, McNutt, Strahan, and Tehranian (2011).
2. Cornett, McNutt, Strahan, and Tehranian (2011).
3. Ojo (2010, December).

4. Schmieder, Hesse, Neudorfer, Puhr, and Schmitz (2012).

5. Basel Committee on Banking Supervision (2010, August).

6. Macroeconomic Assessment Group (2011, October).

7. Macroeconomic Assessment Group (2010, December).

8. Macroeconomic Assessment Group (2010, August).

9. Cornett, McNutt, Strahan, and Tehranian (2011).

10. Basel Committee on Banking Supervision (2010, August).

11. Macroeconomic Assessment Group (2011, October).

12. Macroeconomic Assessment Group (2010, December).

13. Macroeconomic Assessment Group(2010, August).

14. Smit and Pellissier (1997).

15. Cornett, McNutt, Strahan, and Tehranian (2011).

16. Gorton and Metrick (2011).

17. Acharya, Schnabl, and Suarez (2012).

18. Cornett, McNutt, Strahan, and Tehranian (2011).

19. Cornett, McNutt, Strahan, and Tehranian (2011).

20. Schmieder, Hesse, Neudorfer, Puhr, and Schmitz (2012).

21. Ojo (2010, December).

22. Basel Committee on Banking Supervision (2010, August).

23. Macroeconomic Assessment Group (2011, October).

24. Macroeconomic Assessment Group (2010, December).

25. Macroeconomic Assessment Group (2010, August).

26. Basel Committee on Banking Supervision (2010, August).

27. Basel Committee on Banking Supervision (2010, August).

28. Basel Committee on Banking Supervision (2010, August).

29. Basel Committee on Banking Supervision (2010, August).

30. Macroeconomic Assessment Group (2011, October).

31. Macroeconomic Assessment Group (2010, December).

32. Macroeconomic Assessment Group (2010, August).

33. Basel Committee on Banking Supervision (2010, August).

34. Gambacorta (2010).

35. Gambacorta (2010).

36. Gambacorta (2010).

37. EMERG (2013).

38. Cornett, McNutt, Strahan, and Tehranian (2011).

39. Cornett, McNutt, Strahan, and Tehranian (2011).

40. Petersen, De Waal, Hlatshwayo, and Mukuddem-Petersen (2013a).

41. Petersen, De Waal, Hlatshwayo, and Mukuddem-Petersen (2013a).

42. Basel Committee on Banking Supervision (2010).

43. Macroeconomic Assessment Group August (2010).

44. Petersen, De Waal, Mukuddem-Petersen, and Mulaudzi (2012a).

45. Petersen, De Waal, Hlatshwayo, and Mukuddem-Petersen (2013a).

46. Macroeconomic Assessment Group (2011, October).

47. Macroeconomic Assessment Group (2010, December).

48. Macroeconomic Assessment Group (2010, August).

49. Gorton and Metrick (2011).

50. Petersen, De Waal, Mukuddem-Petersen, and Mulaudzi (2012a).

51. Gorton and Metrick (2011).

52. Petersen, De Waal, Mukuddem-Petersen, and Mulaudzi (2012a).

53. Gorton and Metrick (2011).

54. Petersen, De Waal, Mukuddem-Petersen, and Mulaudzi (2012a).

55. Cornett, McNutt, Strahan, and Tehranian (2011).

56. Petersen, Hlatshwayo, Mukuddem-Petersen, and Gideon (2013b).

57. Cornett, McNutt, Strahan, and Tehranian (2011).

58. He and Xiong (2012).

59. Basel Committee on Banking Supervision (2010, August).

60. Macroeconomic Assessment Group (2011, October).

61. Macroeconomic Assessment Group (2010, December).

62. Macroeconomic Assessment Group (2010, August).

63. Petersen, Hlatshwayo, Mukuddem-Petersen, and Gideon (2013b).

64. Macroeconomic Assessment Group (2011, October).

65. Macroeconomic Assessment Group (2010, December).

66. Macroeconomic Assessment Group (2010, August).

67. Macroeconomic Assessment Group (2011, October).

68. Macroeconomic Assessment Group (2010, December).

69. Macroeconomic Assessment Group(2010, August).

70. Macroeconomic Assessment Group (2011, October).

71. Macroeconomic Assessment Group (2010, December).

72. Macroeconomic Assessment Group (2010, August).

73. Macroeconomic Assessment Group (2011, October)

74. Macroeconomic Assessment Group (2010, December).

75. Macroeconomic Assessment Group (2010, August).

76. Macroeconomic Assessment Group (2011, October).

77. Macroeconomic Assessment Group (2010, December).

78. Macroeconomic Assessment Group (2010, August).

79. Macroeconomic Assessment Group (2011, October).

80. Macroeconomic Assessment Group (2010, December).

81. Macroeconomic Assessment Group (2010, August).

82. Macroeconomic Assessment Group (2011, October).

83. Macroeconomic Assessment Group (2010, December).

84. Macroeconomic Assessment Group (2010, August).

References

Acharya, V. V., Gale, D., & Yorulmazer, D. (2011). Rollover risk and market freezes. *Journal of Finance 66*, 1177–1209.

Acharya, V. V., Schnabl, P., & Suarez, G. (2012). Securitization without risk transfer. *Journal of Financial Economics 107*(3), 515–536.

Allen, F., Carletti, E., & Gale, D. (2009). Interbank market liquidity and central bank intervention. *Journal of Monetary Economics 56*, 639–652.

Allen, B., Chan, K. K., Milne, A., & Thomas, S. (2010). *Basel III: Is the cure worse than the disease?* Retrieved April 25, 2013, from http://papers.ssrn.com/sol3/papers.cfm?abstract_id=1688594

Allen, F., & Gale, D. (2004). Financial intermediaries and markets. *Econometrica 72*, 1023–1061.

Allen, F., & Santomero, A. M. (2001). What do financial intermediaries do? *Journal of Banking and Finance 25*, 271–294.

Bank for International Settlements (BIS). (2011, February). *Macroprudential policy tools and frameworks: Update to G20 finance ministers and central bank governors.* BIS Publications. Retrieved April 25, 2012, from http://www.bis.org/publ/othp13.htm

Bank for International Settlements (BIS). (2009, November). *Ten propositions about liquidity crises by Borio C.* (BIS Working Papers No 293). Retrieved July 8, 2013, from http://www.bis.org/publ/work293.pdf

Basel Committee on Banking Supervision (BCBS). (2013, September). *Basel III monitoring report.* Bank for International Settlements (BIS) Publications. Retrieved October 3, 2013, from http://www.bis.org/publ/bcbs262.htm

Basel Committee on Banking Supervision (BCBS). (2013, January). *Liquidity coverage ratio disclosure standards.* Bank for International Settlements (BIS) Publications. Retrieved September 9, 2013, from http://www.bis.org/publ/bcbs259.htm

Basel Committee on Banking Supervision (BCBS). (2013, March). *Results of the Basel III monitoring exercise as of 30 June 2012.* Bank for International Settlements (BIS) Publications. Retrieved October 3, 2013, from http://www.bis.org/publ/bcbs243.htm

Basel Committee on Banking Supervision (BCBS). (2013, January). *Basel III: The liquidity coverage ratio and liquidity risk monitoring tools.* Bank for International Settlements (BIS) Publications. Retrieved June 25, 2013, from http://www.bis.org/publ/bcbs238.htm

Basel Committee on Banking Supervision (2012, September). *Results of the Basel III monitoring exercise as of 31 December 2011.* Bank for International Settlements (BIS) Publications. Retrieved July 25, 2012, from http://www.bis.org/publ/bcbs231.htm

Basel Committee on Banking Supervision (BCBS). (2012, April). *Results of the Basel III monitoring exercise as of 30 June 2011.* Bank for International Settlements (BIS) Publications. Retrieved July 25, 2012, from http://www.bis.org/publ/bcbs217.htm

Basel Committee on Banking Supervision (BCBS). (2011, July). *Basel III framework for liquidity: Frequently asked questions.* Bank for International Settlements (BIS) Publications. Retrieved April 25, 2012, from http://www.bis.org/publ/bcbs199.htm

Basel Committee on Banking Supervision (BCBS). (2011, June). *Basel III: A global regulatory framework for more resilient banks and banking systems—A revised version June 2011.* Bank for International Settlements (BIS) Publications. Retrieved March 25, 2013, from http://www.bis.org/publ/bcbs189.htm

Basel Committee on Banking Supervision (BCBS). (2010b, December). *Basel III: A global regulatory framework for more resilient banks and banking systems.* Bank for International Settlements (BIS) Publications. Retrieved April 25, 2012, from http://www.bis.org/publ/bcbs189.htm

Basel Committee on Banking Supervision (BCBS). (2010a, December). *Basel III: International framework for liquidity risk measurement, standards and monitoring.* Bank for International Settlements (BIS) Publications. Retrieved April 25, 2012, from http://www.bis.org/publ/bcbs188.htm

Basel Committee on Banking Supervision (BCBS). (2010, December). *Results of the comprehensive quantitative impact study.* Bank for International Settlements (BIS) Publications. Retrieved July 25, 2012, from http://www.bis.org/publ/bcbs186.htm

Basel Committee on Banking Supervision (BCBS). (2010, August). *An assessment of the long-term economic impact of stronger capital and liquidity requirements.* Bank for International Settlements (BIS) Publications. Retrieved April 25, 2012, from http://www.bis.org/publ/bcbs175.htm

Basel Committee on Banking Supervision (BCBS). (2009, December). *Consultative document: International framework for liquidity risk measurement, standards and monitoring.* Bank for International Settlements (BIS) Publications. Retrieved April 25, 2012, from http://www.bis.org/publ/bcbs165.htm

Basel Committee on Banking Supervision (BCBS). (2008, September). *Principles for sound liquidity risk management and supervision.* Bank for International Settlements (BIS) Publications. Retrieved April 25, 2012, from http://www.bis.org/publ/bcbs144.htm

Basel Committee on Banking Supervision (BCBS). (2006, June). *Basel II: International convergence of capital measures and capital standards: A revised framework—Comprehensive version.* Bank for International Settlements (BIS) Publications. Retrieved November 21, 2013, from http://www.bis.org/publ/bcbs128.htm

Basel Committee on Banking Supervision (BCBS). (2004, June). *Basel II: International convergence of capital measures and capital standards: A revised framework.* Bank for International Settlements (BIS) Publications. Retrieved November 21, 2013, from http://www.bis.org/publ/bcbs107.htm

Basel Committee on Banking Supervision (BCBS). (1988, July). *International convergence of capital measures and capital standards.* Bank for International Settlements (BIS) Publications. Retrieved November 21, 2013, from http://www.bis.org/publ/bcbs04a.htm

Bureau for Economic Research (BER). (2013). Retrieved October 25, 2013, from http://www.ber.ac.za/

Berger, A. N., & Bouwman, C. H. S. (2012). *Bank liquidity creation, monetary policy and financial crises* (Working paper 2011-041). Philadelphia, PA: Wharton Financial Institutions Center.

Berger, A. N., & Bouwman, C. H. S. (2009). Bank liquidity creation. *Review of Financial Studies 22,* 3779–3837.

Berger, A. N., Bouwman, C. H. S., Kick, T. K., & Schaek, K., (2012). *Bank risk taking and liquidity creation following regulatory interventions and capital support.* Retrieved March 25, 2013, from http://ssrn.com/abstract=1908102

Bernanke, B. S. (1983). Non-monetary effects of the financial crisis in propagation of the Great Depression. *America Economic Review 73,* 257–276.

Bhattacharya, S., & Thakor, A. V. (1993). Contemporary banking theory. *Journal of Financial Intermediation 3,* 2–50.

Brunnermeier, M. K., (2009). Deciphering the liquidity and credit crunch 2007–2008. *Journal of Economic Perspectives 23,* 77–100.

Cornett, M., McNutt, J., Strahan, P., & Tehranian H. (2011). Liquidity risk management and credit supply in the financial crisis. *Journal of Financial Economics 101*(2), 297–312.

Cullen, A. J. (2011, November 10). *Why do banks fail?* Retrieved March 25, 2013, from http://ssrn.com/abstract=1957843

Diamond D. W., & Rajan R. G. (2005). Liquidity shortages and banking crises. *Journal of Finance 60,* 615–647.

Diamond D. W., & Rajan R. G. (2001). Liquidity risk, liquidity creation and financial fragility: A theory of banking. *Journal of Political Economy 109,* 287–327.

Diamond D. W., & Rajan R. G. (2000). A theory of bank capital. *Journal of Finance 55,* 2431–2465.

Distinguin, I., Roulet, C., & Tarazia, A. (2013). *Bank capital buffer and liquidity: Evidence from US and European publicly traded banks.* Retrieved April 13, 2013, from http://ssrn.com/abstract=1884811

European Banking Authority (EBA). (2012, April). *Results of the Basel III monitoring exercise based on data as of 30 June 2011.* EBA Working Paper.

European Banking Authority (EBA). (2012, September). *Results of the Basel III monitoring exercise based on data as of 31 December 2011.* EBA Working Paper.

European Banking Authority (EBA). (2013, April). *Results of the Basel III monitoring exercise based on data as of 30 June 2012.* EBA Working Paper.

European Banking Authority (EBA). (2013, September). *Results of the Basel III monitoring exercise based on data as of 31 December 2012.* EBA Working Paper.

Gambacorta, L. (2010). Do bank capital and liquidity affect real economic activity in the long run? *A VECM analysis for the U.S. Economic Notes (Review of Banking, Finance and Monetary Economics) 40*(3), 75–91.

Garleanu, N., & Pedersen, L. H. (2007). Liquidity and risk management. *American Economic Review 97*, 193–197.

Gorton, G. B., & Metrick, A. (2011). Securitized banking and the run on repo. *Journal of Financial Economics 104*(3), 425–451.

Gorton, G. B., & Winton, A. (2000, October 9). *Liquidity provision, bank capital, and the macroeconomy.* Retrieved March 25, 2013, from http://ssrn.com/abstract=2536849

Granger, C. W. J. (1969). Investigating causal relations by econometric models and cross-spectral methods. *Econometrica 37*(3), 424–438.

Gu, T. (2011). *Procyclicality of the Basel II credit risk measurements and the improvements in Basel III.* Aarhus, Denmark: Aarhus School of Business, Aarhus University.

He, Z., & Xiong, W. (2012). Rollover risk and credit risk. *Journal of Finance 67*, 391–429.

Hong, H., Huang, J., & Wu, D. (2013). *The information content of Basel III liquidity risk measures* (Working Paper, p. 46).

Horvath, R., Seidler, J., & Weill, L. (2012). *Bank capital and liquidity creation: Granger-causality evidence* (Working paper series No. 1497).

Institute of International Finance (IIF). (2010, June). *Interim report on the cumulative impact on the global economy of proposed changes in the banking regulatory framework.* Washingto, DC: Institue of International Finance.

Kullback, S. (1959). *Information theory and statistics.* New York, NY: Wiley.

Larson, J. (2011, April). *The Basel Capital Accords.* Working Paper, University of Iowa.

MacKinnon, J. G. (1996). Numerical distribution functions for unit root and cointegration tests. *Journal of Applied Econometrics 11*, 601–618.

Macroeconomic Assessment Group (MAG). (2010, August). *Assessing the macroeconomic impact of the transition to stronger capital and liquidity requirements.* Interim report, Group established by the Financial Stability Board and the BCBS.

Macroeconomic Assessment Group (MAG). (2010, December). *Assessing the macroeconomic impact of the transition to stronger capital and liquidity requirements* (Final report). Retrieved March 25, 2010, from http://www.bis.org/publ/othp12.htm

Macroeconomic Assessment Group (MAG). (2011, October). *Assessment of the macroeconomic impact of higher loss absorbency for global systemically important banks* (BIS report). Retrieved March 25, 2013, from http://www.bis.org/publ/bcbs202.htm

Chabanel, P.E. (2012). *Basel III regulatory update.* Retrieved on June 7, 2012, from http://www.moodysanalytics.com/~/media/Insight/Regulatory/Basel-III/Presentations/2012-13-06-Basel-III-Regulatory-Update.ashx

Ojo, M. (2010, December). *Preparing for Basel IV—Why liquidity risks still present a challenge to regulators in prudential supervision.* Retrieved April 25, 2012, from http://ssrn.com/abstract=1729057

Petersen, M. A., De Waal, B., Hlatshwayo, L. N. P., & Mukuddem-Petersen, J. (2013a). A note on Basel III and liquidity. *Applied Economic Letters 20*(8), 777–780.

Petersen, M. A., Hlatshwayo L. N. P., Mukuddem-Petersen, J., & Gideon, F. (2013b). Economics of Debt. Series: Economics. In *Basel III and liquidity* (Chapter 10, pp. 237–316). New York, NY: Nova Science Publishers.

Petersen, M. A., De Waal, B., Mukuddem-Petersen, J., & Mulaudzi, M. P. (2014). Subprime mortgage funding and liquidity risk. *Quantitative Finance 5*(3), 545–555.

Petersen, M. A., Senosi M. C., & Mukuddem-Petersen, J. (2012b). *Subprime Mortgage Models. Book Series: Banking and Banking Developments.* New York, NY: Nova Science

EMERG. (2013). *2002–2012 EMERG global banking data.* Retrieved November 4, 2013, from http://emerg.com/global/liquidity/data

Repullo, R. (2004). Capital requirements, market power and risk-taking in banking. *Journal of Financial Intermediation 13*, 156–182.

Schmieder, C., Hesse, H., Neudorfer, B., Puhr, C., & Schmitz, S. W. (2012, January). *Next generation system-wide liquidity stress testing* (IMF Working Paper WP/12/3). Monetary and Capital Markets Department.

Smit, B. W., & Pellissier, G. M. (1997). The BER annual econometric model of the South African economy: A cointegration version. *Journal for Studies in Economics and Econometrics 21*(1), 1–35.

Thomas, L. C., Edelman, D. B., & Crook, J. N. (2002). *Credit Scoring and its Applications.* Philadelphia, PA: Society for Industrial and Applied Mathematics.

Thornton, D. C. (2009, May). What the Libor-Ois spread says. *Economic Synopses 24*, Retrieved April 25, 2013, from http://www.stlouis.fed.org.

Wu, D. & Hong, H. (2012a). *The information value of Basel III liquidity risk measures*. Retrieved December 21, 2012, from http://ssrn.com/abstract=1729057

Wu, D. & Hong, H. (2012b). *Liquidity risk, market valuation, and bank failures* (Working Paper). Office of the Comptroller of the Currency and Stanford University.

Index

OTHER TITLES FROM THE ECONOMICS COLLECTION

Philip Romero, The University of Oregon and Jeffrey Edwards,
North Carolina A&T State University, Editors

- *Managerial Economics: Concepts and Principles* by Donald Stengel
- *Your Macroeconomic Edge: Investing Strategies for the Post-Recession World* by Philip J. Romero
- *Working with Economic Indicators: Interpretation and Sources* by Donald Stengel
- *Innovative Pricing Strategies to Increase Profits* by Daniel Marburger
- *Regression for Economics* by Shahdad Naghshpour
- *Statistics for Economics* by Shahdad Naghshpour
- *How Strong Is Your Firm's Competitive Advantage?* by Daniel Marburger
- *A Primer on Microeconomics* by Thomas Beveridge
- *Game Theory: Anticipating Reactions for Winning Actions* by Mark L. Burkey
- *A Primer on Macroeconomics* by Thomas Beveridge
- *Economic Decision Making Using Cost Data: A Guide for Managers* by Daniel Marburger
- *The Fundamentals of Money and Financial Systems* by Shahdad Naghshpour
- *International Economics: Understanding the Forces of Globalization for Managers* by Paul Torelli
- *The Economics of Crime* by Zagros Madjd-Sadjadi
- *Money and Banking: An Intermediate Market-Based Approach* by William D. Gerdes

Announcing the Business Expert Press Digital Library

*Concise E-books Business Students Need
for Classroom and Research*

This book can also be purchased in an e-book collection by your library as
- a one-time purchase,
- that is owned forever,
- allows for simultaneous readers,
- has no restrictions on printing, and
- can be downloaded as PDFs from within the library community.

Our digital library collections are a great solution to beat the rising cost of textbooks. e-books can be loaded into their course management systems or onto student's e-book readers.

The **Business Expert Press** digital libraries are very affordable, with no obligation to buy in future years. For more information, please visit **www.businessexpertpress.com/librarians**. To set up a trial in the United States, please email **sales@businessexpertpress.com**.

www.ingramcontent.com/pod-product-compliance
Lightning Source LLC
Chambersburg PA
CBHW060558210326
41519CB00014B/3509